Restaurant Accounting with QuickBooks

How to set up and use QuickBooks to manage
your restaurant finances

Second Edition

by

Doug Sleeter and Stacey L. Byrne, CPA

Published by

The Sleeter Group

A Division of Diversified Business Communications

Restaurant Accounting with QuickBooks®

How to set up and use QuickBooks to manage your restaurant finances

Second Edition

Doug Sleeter and Stacey L. Byrne, CPA

Copyright © 2015 by Diversified Business Communications

All Rights Reserved

Published by The Sleeter Group, a Diversified Communications company

POS Chapter Contributed by Joe Aliota

Reviewed by Robyn Smithson

ISBN: Printed Edition: 978-1-942417-12-5   Ebook Edition: 978-1-942417-11-8

Published in the United States by The Sleeter Group, Inc.

888-484-5484 www.sleeter.com

Twitter: @sleetergroup

Facebook: The-Sleeter-Group

Version 2015.1

Dedication

This book is dedicated to my "Uncle Sid" Willeford, who recently left this earth. He is the reason I developed this book. Sid created the most awesome restaurant experience in the world, Fiamma Cucina Rustica, located in Tahoe City, California. I've never had a better dining experience than at Fiamma, and it was all because of his creative vision for what a restaurant should be. It was an honor and a privilege to help him with his restaurant accounting system; and now I hope to help thousands of other restaurant owners around the world with this book. Rest in Peace, Sid.

Doug Sleeter

Dedication

This book is dedicated to my two sons, Robert P. Byrne and John Ryan Byrne. I love you both with all of my heart. Never forget the famous quote by Walt Disney, "Dreams can come true if we have the courage to pursue them."

Stacey Byrne

Restaurant Accounting with QuickBooks

Contents

Preface

Thanks for choosing this book to learn about managing restaurant accounting using QuickBooks.

This is a guide to the specific setup and usage of QuickBooks desktop software for everyday restaurant accounting. We provide an overview of most of the aspects of business management with QuickBooks, with a deep dive into other aspects. The material in this book assumes you have some familiarity with how to navigate around and use QuickBooks for Windows. Most "how to use QuickBooks" topics not covered in detail in this book can be found in our *QuickBooks Complete Textbook* at The Sleeter Group's online store (store.sleeter.com), as well as in articles found in the Sleeter Report blog (sleeter.com/blog), an online magazine.

This book shows you how to use QuickBooks to:

- Set Preferences to optimize the functionality of QuickBooks

- Set up or import your Chart of Accounts

- Set up Items so QuickBooks handles the behind the scenes accounting

- Use the Sales Rep List to track sales by server

- Set up Customers, Custom Fields, and Vendor Type Lists

- Customize and manage Templates

- Account for credit card tips collected and paid in cash to servers

- Customize QuickBooks payroll for use with restaurants, including collecting payroll taxes on cash and credit card tips previously paid to employees and what to do if you encounter negative paychecks

- Set up and record daily sales entries using end-of-day summary reports (or Z-tapes) from your Point of Sale (POS) system

- Managing house charges, or "on account" charges, invoices, statements, and payments

- Record bank deposits, separating various credit cards and check/cash deposits and grouping deposits so the bank reconciliation goes smoothly

- Set up vendors, track 1099 information, manage accounts payable bills and bill payments, apply vendor credits, and write, print, and void checks

- Track cash paid out of the register

- Use Bill.com to manage the bill payment process

- Track company credit cards

- Manage sales tax

- Adjust inventory based on physical counts

- Reconcile bank statements, including tips for locating bank reconciliation discrepancies and using bank feeds

- Track company credit card charges and reconcile credit card statements

- Customize, memorize, and print common reports for managing the restaurant

- Understand information presented on the financial statements

This book also includes a chapter on what to consider when selecting a POS system.

A sample restaurant QuickBooks data file is available that can be used to export lists and templates that can be used to set up a restaurant business with QuickBooks from scratch. The restaurant sample file is all set up with the recommended Chart of Accounts, Items, Sales Receipt Templates, Memorized Reports, and other lists that give restaurant owners and managers a complete back-office financial system.

This system will work with any cash register or POS system because it works independently and does not require a direct link with the POS system.

You'll learn detailed instructions for entering daily sales totals for each server into QuickBooks at the end of each shift. With just a single QuickBooks entry for each server each day, this system helps you track everything you need for most of your restaurant accounting.

How to Use This Book

The methods presented in the book (including the screenshots) will work with the desktop version of QuickBooks Pro, Premier, or Enterprise. The screen shots are taken from the restaurant sample file, which is in QuickBooks 2015 Premier format, but many of the techniques apply to any version of QuickBooks.

Assuming you are using QuickBooks for Windows, there are three ways to approach your learning with this book:

1. You can read the book and set up your own company file using the methods presented here, or

2. You can restore the sample company file (AcademyRestaurant2015.QBM) and learn how it works by reading the book and practicing in QuickBooks, or

3. You can create a new file, export the lists and templates from the restaurant sample file, and import the lists and templates into your own QuickBooks file as shown in Appendix A.

You can use some of the concepts here with QuickBooks Online or QuickBooks for Mac, but several changes to the set up will be needed and the screenshots will not match. We do not go into any detail on how the methods described in this book differ from QuickBooks Online or QuickBooks for Mac. You can use this book as a guide and develop your own workflow to adapt features that may not be present in other versions of QuickBooks.

Using the Restaurant Sample File

The Restaurant Accounting with QuickBooks Sample File is a portable QuickBooks file named *AcademyRestaurant2015.QBM*. Please visit www.sleeter.com/downloads and select this book's title from the drop down menu to download these files. When you download the restaurant sample file, save it in a folder on your computer where you'll be able to find and restore it later.

The file is compatible with the following QuickBooks versions:

- QuickBooks Pro or Premier, version 2015 or later

- QuickBooks Enterprise version 15 or later

Restore the Sample File

To restore the restaurant sample company file and experiment with the topics and methods covered in this book, open QuickBooks and follow these steps:

1. Select **Open or Restore Company**... from the *File* Menu.

2. Select **Restore a portable file.**

3. Find the **AcademyRestaurant2015.QBM** file you downloaded on your local hard drive and select it. Click **Open**.

4. When prompted to save your **AcademyRestaurant2015.QBW** file, navigate to the desired folder and click **Save**.

When you're ready to go live with your own company file, you can simply create a new file, export lists and templates from the restaurant sample file, and import them in to the new file as described in Appendix A

Chapter 1
Introduction

A restaurant's success relies on an effective back office accounting system, and QuickBooks financial software can be a critical part of that success. QuickBooks can be used for purchasing, bill paying, gift certificate tracking, cash management, time tracking, and payroll. However, restaurants that choose QuickBooks for their accounting will need to understand how to properly set up and use QuickBooks to meet their unique needs.

This book will guide you through this process.

Restaurant Accounting – The Big Picture

If your restaurant is like most restaurants, there are one or more cash registers or Point of Sale (POS) terminals that ring up each sale during the business day. At the end of each day, this information should be entered into QuickBooks through a *Sales Receipt* that records the summary information from the cash register or POS system. This book will show you how to use the end-of-day report (sometimes called the Z-tape) from the POS system to record just a few simple transactions each day in QuickBooks that will handle all of the day-to-day accounting in your restaurant.

Although there are several POS systems that provide a direct integration (software connection) with QuickBooks, this book assumes your cash register is not integrated with QuickBooks.

Throughout this book, we use the restaurant sample file available to you as discussed on page ix. Keep in mind that this book offers one approach for how you can quickly and easily set up and track your restaurant financial system in QuickBooks; however, if it's not a perfect match for your situation, you can modify it for your specific needs.

Other Considerations

Desktop vs. Online Accounting

Traditional QuickBooks Desktop software lives on your local computer or local network and can only be accessed by people in the same office or on the same network. This works well for businesses that don't need to share the data file (in which all accounting data is stored) with anyone outside of the office.

If multiple people who are not located in the same physical location need access to the bookkeeping data – such as the restaurant owner, outside bookkeeper, Certified Public Accountant, or other accounting professional – the traditional desktop software presents problems. The first issue is that only one person at a time can add transactions into the data file. So when the accountant needs to work on the file – for example when making adjusting entries for tax – nobody else can be recording new data in the file. The next problem is that the data file has to be moved from computer to computer by sending backups back and forth. This can get very messy. By moving the file around, someone could accidentally, or without full understanding, continue to work in the file that they have copied and given to someone else to work on. When the file comes back and is restored to the local computer, a loss of data may occur if both people were working on different copies of the file. Even when things go perfectly, this process is cumbersome and complicated for most "normal people."

There are online accounting programs in the marketplace that are designed to remove the inconvenience caused by the physical transfer of the data file by providing access to the file online. QuickBooks Online, Xero, and Sage One are examples of online accounting product providers. With an online accounting program, the data file lives "in the cloud," which means it lives on the software company's server and can be accessed from anywhere using an Internet connection. Many of these products even allow access from an iPad or with an app that works on your cell phone.

With all of the benefits of the cloud, you might be wondering why we're writing a book about how to use QuickBooks *for the desktop* to run your restaurant. Well, over time, we do plan to write similar books using cloud and mobile solutions, but as we write this in 2015, we conclude that we can achieve more efficiencies for your core accounting, bookkeeping, and sales tax reporting needs by using the desktop version of QuickBooks than by utilizing any of the other options we are aware of today. The issue with the newer products is that they lack the features (sometimes very tiny features such as zero-dollar sales receipts, payment items, and sales reps) that allow us to streamline your restaurant accounting system without requiring you to overcomplicate your processes.

As the online products continue to evolve and new features are added, these differences in functionality should continue to decrease and make the online products more attractive. For now, we believe the restaurant industry is best served by using the traditional QuickBooks for Windows desktop products.

QuickBooks Desktop with Benefits of Online Access

What if we could use QuickBooks for Windows, but still access it from anywhere at any time via the Internet? Well, there is some good news here, even though it adds a bit of extra cost to the overall solution. By having the QuickBooks Desktop software "hosted" on a virtual server, you can provide multiple users with concurrent access to the same data file from different physical locations.

Intuit provides a list of authorized QuickBooks hosting providers on their website at http://www.intuithostingprogram.com/authorized_hosts.php. Hosting is a great solution, but you can expect to pay between $25 and $70 per user per month for this solution. It could definitely be worth it when you consider all the benefits.

For more information on using a hosting provider, see the article *Moving to Hosted Virtual Servers* posted in the *Sleeter Report*.

Chapter 2
Setting up QuickBooks for Restaurants

The restaurant sample file discussed earlier can be downloaded to your local computer (or your hosted virtual server) and restored to a QuickBooks company file, as discussed on page x. You can test out the concepts and repeat the same structure in your own company file. You can also use the methods described in Appendix A to create a file from scratch and use the restaurant sample file to export lists and templates.

Whether you are using the restaurant sample file or starting a file from scratch, you should be familiar with setting preferences, creating various *Items*, and setting up sales forms in QuickBooks.

QuickBooks Preferences

There are two types of *Preferences* in QuickBooks:

1. **User Preferences (My Preferences).** User Preferences are specific to the user who is currently logged on to the QuickBooks company file. A user can make changes to his or her Preferences as desired. These preferences are located under the *My Preferences* tab for each preference.

2. **Company Preferences**. Company Preferences make global changes to the features and functionality of a company's data file. Only the *Administrator* of the data file can make changes to Company Preferences.

In this section, you will learn about a few of these *Preferences* and how they affect QuickBooks. There are several categories of *Preferences* that you can explore on your own. Clicking the **Help** button in the *Preferences* window will launch QuickBooks Help, with specific topics relevant to the *Preference* in the open window.

To access QuickBooks Preferences, click **Edit > Preferences**. The categories of preferences you can edit are listed along the left side of the *Preferences* window. Additional information about the preferences is shown below.

Accounting – Company Preferences

Click **Accounting** on the left side of the *Preferences* window and click the *Company Preferences* tab. The administrator can set the following preferences for all users:

- Turn on account numbers by clicking *Use account numbers* (recommended).

- Turn on class tracking, if desired, by clicking *Use class tracking for transactions*. This is useful if you have multiple locations and want to track sales and expenses for each location. In this book, we will not be covering class tracking.

- *Automatically assign general journal entry number.*

- Set various warnings when posting transactions.

- Set a closing date through which the books are closed by clicking *Set Date/Password*. Choosing this option will require users to enter the password that you set in order to post transactions to the closed period.

Figure 2-1 Accounting Preferences, Company Preferences

Desktop View – User Preferences

The user preferences for *Desktop View* allow each user to customize the default windows that show when they open QuickBooks, including:

- Viewing one window or multiple windows. The default setting is for *Multiple Windows* as shown in Figure 2-2. If this preference is changed to *One Window,* you will not be able to display more than one QuickBooks window at a time, and you will not be able to change the size of QuickBooks windows.

- The *Show Home page when opening a company file* option causes the *Home* page window to be displayed whenever the company file is opened. This can be turned on or off at each user's discretion.

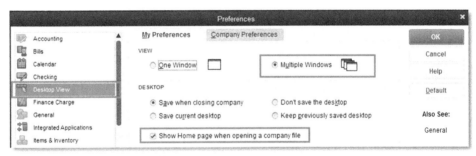

Figure 2-2 Desktop View, User Preferences

- The *Company File Color Scheme* option allows each user to choose the background color that is shown. This is particularly helpful if you have multiple QuickBooks files and need to easily determine which file you are in based on the background color.

> **Tip:**
> If you use QuickBooks in a multi-user environment, it may be best to select the **Don't save the desktop** radio button in the user preferences. If you save the desktop, each time you open QuickBooks it will re-open all of the windows and reports you were viewing when you last used the program. If you save the desktop, this may negatively impact performance for other users when they open the data file.

Desktop View – Company Preferences

The *Company Preferences* tab in the *Desktop View* area controls which icons display on the *Home* page. These settings can only be changed by the *Administrator* and will affect every user who uses this company file. You can remove some icons from displaying on the *Home* page. However, turning off the icon on the *Home* page does not disable the feature, since you can still access the command using the menus.

Some features, such as *Estimates, Sales Tax,* and *Sales Orders* listed in the *Related Preferences* section can only be removed from the *Home* page by disabling the feature using the appropriate *Preferences*. You can enable or disable these features by clicking on the name of the feature in the *Desktop View* company preferences window. You will be redirected to the appropriate preference area where you can turn the feature on or off.

The default settings in *Desktop View* company preferences should look like Figure 2-3.

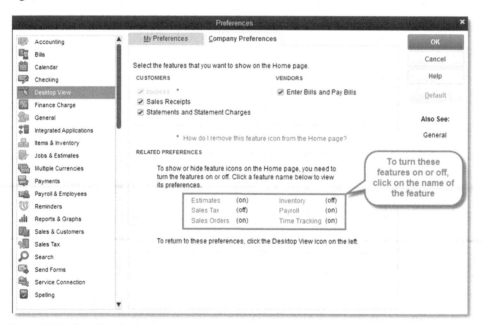

Figure 2-3 Desktop View Preferences

> **Note:**
> If your restaurant allows some customers to pay on credit (i.e., if you have "house accounts") as described in Chapter 6, you should check the **Statements and Statement Charges** checkbox so you can create *Statements* from the *Home* page. If you don't send statements to customers, you can uncheck this preference.

General Preferences – User Preferences

The *My Preferences* tab in the *General* area offers several choices for each user, as shown in Figure 2-4.

With the *Preferences* window still open, click **General** on the left and then click the **My Preferences** tab at the top.

- If you prefer not to use the Tab key to move around within forms, you can choose **Pressing Enter moves between fields** and the "Enter" key will move you from field to field on the form.

- By default, QuickBooks "beeps" every time you record a transaction. If you prefer, turn off the "beep" by unchecking the box for **Beep when recording a transaction**.

- If you prefer not to enter in a decimal point when entering numbers, check the box for **Automatically place decimal point** and QuickBooks will interpret 10000 as 100.00 without having to enter the decimal.

- **Keep QuickBooks running for quick startups** should be left unchecked. This was designed to help QuickBooks open faster. However, when this box is checked, a portion of the QuickBooks keeps running in memory when you exit, which can affect performance of other programs. This may be especially problematic when third party add-on programs are being used.

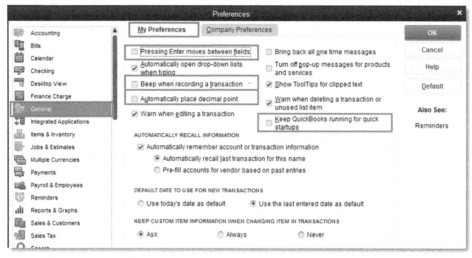

Figure 2-4 General, User Preferences

General Preferences - Company Preferences

There are a few *General* preferences in the *Company Preferences* tab. For example, you can choose whether time entries are shown as a decimal (e.g., 8.50 for ½ past 8, or with a colon to show minutes; or 8:30 for 8 hours and 30 minutes). QuickBooks defaults to minutes. You may or may not need to change this setting, depending on your timekeeping system reports.

Other defaults are *Always show year as 4 digits* and *Save transactions before printing.* We recommend you keep these defaults.

It is important to change the default for *Never update name information when saving transactions* from unchecked to checked. You will understand the implications of this change in Chapter 6, starting on page 71.

Your *General Company Preferences* should look like Figure 2-5.

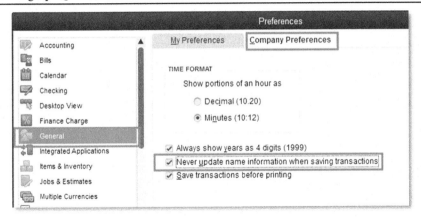

Figure 2-5 General, Company Preferences

Payments – Company Preferences

The *Payments Preferences* settings shown in Figure 2-6 determine how QuickBooks handles payment receipts, as discussed in the Managing House Accounts chapter.

The *Automatically apply payments* and *Automatically calculate payments* preferences relate to whether or not you are invoicing customers or sending out statements and receiving payments later. If you are not managing house accounts, these two preferences are not applicable. If you are managing house accounts you will want to leave these checked.

In order for QuickBooks to allow for batching and grouping deposits, the *Use Undeposited Funds as a default deposit to account* needs to be checked as shown in Figure 2-6.

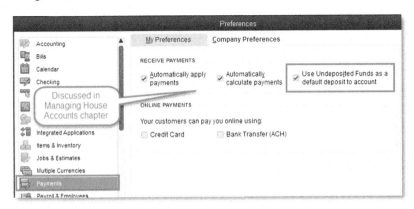

Figure 2-6 Payments, Company Preferences

Reports & Graphs – Company Preferences

QuickBooks allows you to customize information on reports and graphs. You can choose whether you want reports to print on an accrual or cash basis and also choose how you want *Accounts* and *Items* to print on reports. In addition, you can change the default formatting for reports in the *Company Preferences* tab.

If you plan to use *Accounts Payable* or *Accounts Receivable Aging* reports, as discussed later in this book, we recommend that you choose the option to **Age from due date**, as shown in Figure 2-7.

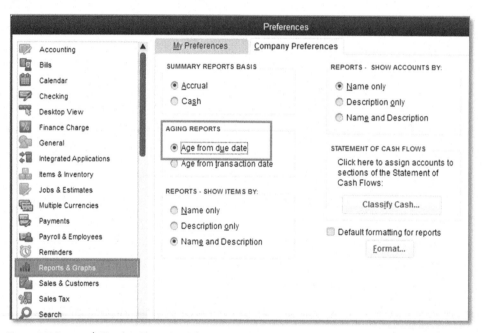

Figure 2-7 Reports & Graphs, Company Preferences

> **Note:**
> The *Reports–Show Items By* section of the company preferences tab determines whether the name, description, or both are shown on reports. The restaurant sample file is set to show *Name only*. Depending on your preferences, you may want to include descriptions that are entered when *Accounts* and *Items* are set up.

Sales Tax – Company Preferences

In order for QuickBooks to manage the collection and payment of sales taxes, you will need to turn on the sales tax feature, as shown in Figure 2-8.

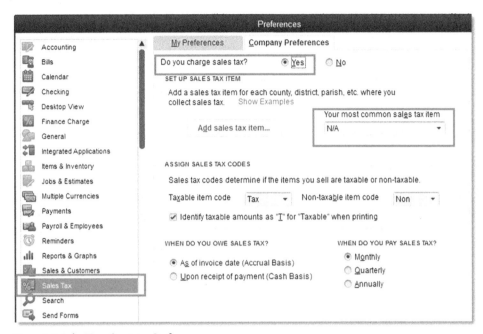

Figure 2-8 Sales Tax, Company Preferences

The *Your most common sales tax item* will be completed after you set up the items discussed later in this chapter. If you have imported the *Items List* from the restaurant sample file, the **N/A** tax item will already be available to select.

> **Note:**
> The *Sales Tax Item* listed in the *Your most common sales tax item* field becomes the default sales tax item on new customer records, as well as on *Sales Receipts* and *Invoices*.

The *When Do You Owe Sales Tax?* box defaults to *Accrual Basis*. This is the most common scenario. Generally speaking, cash basis taxpayers are required to remit sales tax on an accrual basis. Since restaurants are not usually carrying taxable sales in Accounts Receivable, this should not be an issue, but if you're a cash basis taxpayer, you should consider this setting and discuss it with your tax advisor.

Time & Expenses – Company Preferences

Use this window to turn on time tracking and ensure that the first day of the workweek is set according to your workweek. This will allow the timesheets in QuickBooks to be displayed correctly. If the pay period ends on Saturday, change the setting to *Sunday*. The use of timesheets to prepare payroll checks is discussed in Chapter 4.

Since restaurants don't typically invoice customers for employee time, uncheck the box for *Mark all time entries as billable*. Similarly, since restaurants don't typically invoice customers for expenses incurred, uncheck the box for *Mark all expenses as billable*.

The *Time & Expenses* Company Preferences should match Figure 2-9.

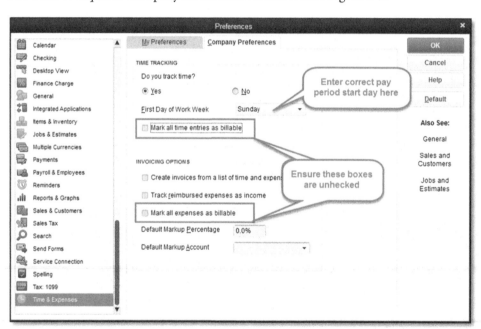

Figure 2-9 Time & Expenses, Company Preferences

Chart of Accounts

A complete *Chart of Accounts* list is included in the restaurant sample file with many of the accounts you will need for a restaurant. The list is fully customizable and can be changed to suit your specific needs.

Industry-Specific Accounts

A few restaurant-specific accounts are needed in order for you to manage the transactions and create the reports we recommend. Selected Balance Sheet accounts are shown in Figure 2-10 and discussed in detail below.

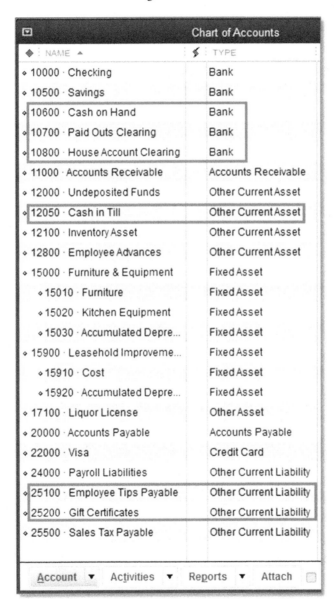

Figure 2-10 Selected Balance Sheet Accounts

The *Cash on Hand* account is used to account for cash paid out to servers each night at the end of their shift. It is designated in QuickBooks as a *Bank* account, but it is not a real bank account. It is a "drawer" or "safe" on the premises that will be used to pay out cash to servers for tips collected by credit card. Periodically, the manager of the restaurant should replenish the cash in this drawer so there is always enough cash on hand to pay tips to the servers. This replenishment can be done by holding cash back from your bank deposits or by cashing a check at your bank. Make the check payable to "Cash" and use *Cash on Hand* as the expense account.

Clearing accounts are holding accounts that are designed to "clear" out the balance on a regular basis. In this book we will use the following clearing accounts:

- *Paid Outs Clearing* – This is a virtual *Bank* account used to account for cash that is paid out of the register. This is discussed in detail in Chapter 8 – Managing Expenses, and is different from the *Cash on Hand* fund used to pay out tips.

- *House Accounts Clearing* – This is a virtual *Bank* account used to account for customers who have been given the privilege of charging their meals on a house account and paying for them weekly or monthly. This is discussed in detail in Chapter 6 – Managing House Accounts.

- *Employee Tips Payable* – This is an *Other Current Liability* account used to account for tips received on credit cards and paid out to servers in cash. This is discussed in detail in Chapter 5 – Recording Daily Sales The *Cash in Till* account is where the initial starting till amounts are tracked as an asset. If the restaurant has 5 tills that start each day with $300 in change, the *Cash in Till* account would have a $1,500 balance. This amount will generally not change unless more tills are added or the amount in each till changes. If the restaurant decides to increase each of the 5 tills to $400, write a check to cash using *Cash in Till* as the expense account for the $500 ($100 each times 5 tills).

The *Gift Certificates* account is used to track gift certificates sold and redeemed. Setting up *Items* to track Gift Certificate sales and redemptions is discussed on page 25.

The *Income* and *Cost of Goods Sold* accounts in the restaurant sample file are suggested for a typical restaurant, but you can modify these accounts to fit your needs, as discussed on page 17. You can decide how much detail you want to see in the income and cost of goods sold sections. If you want to track profitability for food versus bar sales, you should ensure that all sales recorded use *Items* that point to the correct account, and ensure that payments for food and beverages are properly categorized.

The *Expense* accounts are similar to most businesses, with a few additional accounts such as *Marketing Expense – Complimentary Food & Beverage, Uniforms* and *Linen Expense*.

Customizing the Chart of Accounts

It is easy to customize the *Chart of Accounts* in QuickBooks by using the buttons shown at the bottom of Figure 2-11 to add, edit, or delete accounts.

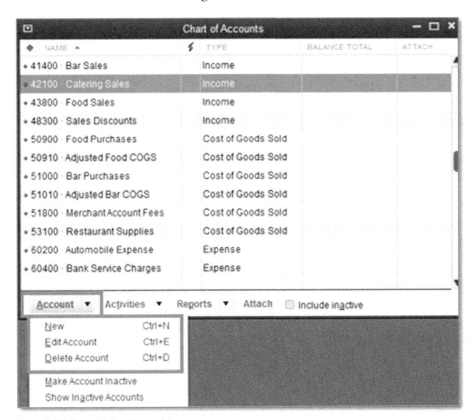

Figure 2-11 Customizing Chart of Accounts

Deleting Accounts

To delete accounts that you do not need, follow these steps:

1.   Click on **Lists** > **Chart of Accounts**.

2.   Click on the name of the account you want to delete to highlight it.

3.   Select **Account** in the lower left corner.

4.   Choose **Delete**.

5.   If the account has never been used in transactions or in list items, QuickBooks will ask you to confirm deletion.

6.   Click **OK** to delete the undesired account.

> **Tip:**
> Notice that on the right side of the commands in Figure 2-11, there is a *Ctrl+D* listed next to *Delete*. This is shortcut that will allow you to highlight the account you want to delete; press **Ctrl+D** to delete the account without selecting Account > Delete Account. These shortcuts are listed in several places in QuickBooks and can help save you keystrokes and mouse clicks.

Adding Accounts and Using Subaccounts

If you would like to add accounts that are not listed in the sample *Chart of Accounts*, create your own list from scratch, or create a list based on the National Restaurant Association's Chart of Accounts, use the following steps:

1.   Click on Lists > Chart of Accounts.

2.   Select **Account** in the lower left corner.

3.   Choose **Add**.

4.   Alternatively, you can open the *Chart of Accounts* and press the keyboard shortcut **Ctrl+A** to add a new account.

5.   The *Add New Account* window will open prompting you to choose an account type as shown in Figure 2-12.

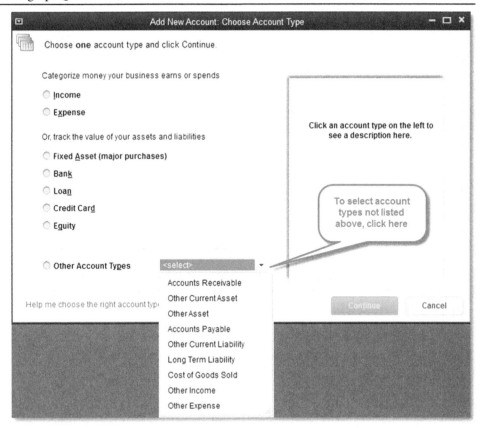

Figure 2-12 Add New Account, Choose Account Type

6.   Choose the correct account type for the account you are adding and click
      Continue.

7.   Enter in an account number (if this *Accounting Preference* is turned on as
      discussed on page 6).

8.   Enter in the Account Name.

9.   Notice the check box for *Subaccount of* under the *Account Name*. This
      allows for grouping accounts together that you want to see totaled on
      reports.

To add an account for *Wine Sales* and include the amounts with other sales in
the *Bar Sales* account, complete the *Income* account setup as shown in Figure
2-13.

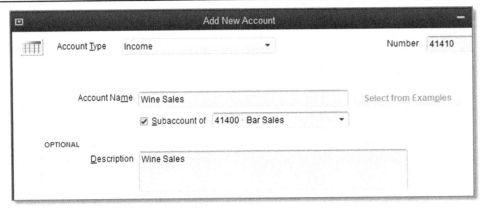

Figure 2-13 Chart of Accounts, Adding Subaccount

Using subaccounts gives you great flexibility in grouping *Items* by category, including Staffing Costs, Occupancy Costs, Direct Operating Expenses, Marketing Expenses, and other desired groups of expenses. When benchmarking your restaurant expenses against industry standards, it may be helpful to include all of your *Occupancy Costs* in one category for analysis purposes, while maintaining the individual categories of Rent, Property Taxes, and Insurance on the Property for tax purposes. With subaccounts, you can accomplish both goals.

Editing Accounts

To modify the *Account Type, Name* or *Account Number* for existing accounts, follow these steps:

1. Click on **Lists** > **Chart of Accounts**.

2. Click on the name of the account you want to edit to highlight it.

3. Select **Account** in the lower left corner.

4. Choose **Edit**.

5. Alternatively, you can open the *Chart of Accounts,* highlight the account to edit and press the keyboard shortcut **Ctrl+E** to edit the account.

6. Make the desired changes.

7. Click **Save & Close**.

Items for Restaurants

Understanding *Items* is key to understanding how QuickBooks works. *Items* "teach" the software about which accounts are used in each transaction you enter on forms, such as sales receipts, invoices, checks, and so on. By giving each item a useful name and connecting it to the appropriate accounts in the Chart of Accounts, QuickBooks automatically handles the debits and credits behind the scenes.

The most important step in getting your restaurant accounting to work efficiently is to create the proper *Items*, as shown in this section. If the workflows described in this book don't apply to your particular restaurant, we hope that by giving you explanations of what each QuickBooks *Item Type* is doing behind the scenes, you will be able to adapt and modify *Items* to suit your needs.

Figure 2-14 illustrates the *Items List* for a typical restaurant. Each *Item Type* (Service, Other Charge, Subtotal, Discount, Payment, and Sales Tax Items) determines how the transactional entries will behave on sales forms and reports. It is important to select the proper *Item Type* when setting up your *Items List*. This will be discussed in more detail in the sections below.

Figure 2-14 Item list for Restaurants

Sales Tax Codes

In order for QuickBooks to help you differentiate things that are reported as taxable and non-taxable sales (like tips collected), *Sales Tax Codes* are used and added to the daily *Sales Receipt* entries. You will see how this works in Chapter 5 – Recording Daily Sales . *Tax* and *Non* are already set up for you when you turn on the sales tax feature. To add the **EX** code for *Items* that are excluded from sales tax reporting, as shown in the restaurant sample file, follow these steps:

1.   Click on **Lists > Sales Tax Code List**.

2.   Select **Sales Tax Code** in the lower left corner and choose **New**.

Complete the *New Sales Tax Code* window by entering the codes shown in Figure 2-15.

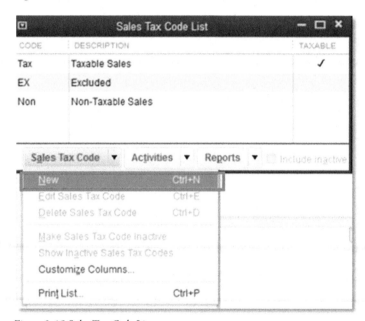

Figure 2-15 Sales Tax Code List

Items You Sell

Use the *Service* item type to set up the *Items* you sell, including:

- Food Sales

- Bar Sales

The sales *Items* are included on sales reports and are the *Items* that feed the sales tax liability report. You can review these items in the restaurant sample file.

To begin setting up *Items*, follow these steps:

1. Click on **Lists > Items List**. Alternatively, you can click on the **Items and Services** icon on the *Home* page in the upper right corner.

2. Select **Item** in the lower left corner and then select **New**.

3. Complete the *New Item* window as described below, depending on the type of item you are creating.

4. Enter in a *description*.

5. Leave the *rate* field blank.

6. Enter in the appropriate *tax code* for this item (taxable, non-taxable, or excluded).

7. Enter in the appropriate *account* that you want QuickBooks to connect this item to. The *Food Sales* item is linked to the *Food Sales* account.

Figure 2-16 shows the setup for the *Food Sales* item.

> **Note:**
> In Figure 2-14 there is a single item called *Food Sales* and another for *Bar Sales*. You can create more *Items* if you want to track more detailed sales information. You may decide to track *Taxable Food Sales* and *Non Taxable Food Sales*. Each orderable item on the menu could be a separate *Item* in your *Item List*, but if this information is being provided by your point of sale system, you may not need this level of detail in the QuickBooks file. It depends on the level of sales reporting you want QuickBooks to provide.

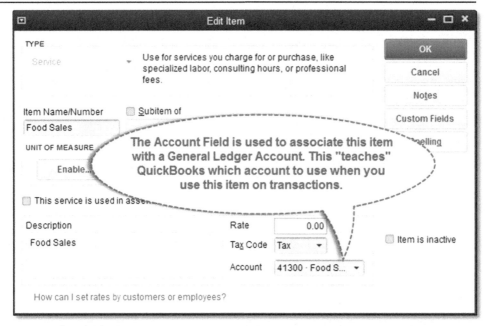

Figure 2-16 Food Sales, Service Item

Subtotal Item

Create a *Subtotal* type item called **Subtotal** as shown in Figure 2-17. The proper placement of this subtotal on the daily *Sales Receipt* will have an impact on the sales tax reports. We will discuss proper placement and sales tax reports later in the book.

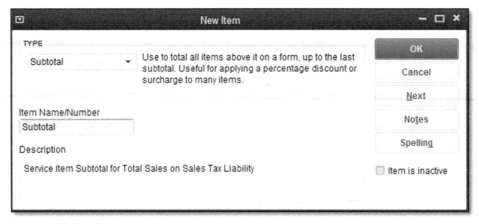

Figure 2-17 Subtotal Item

Gift Certificates

When you sell a gift certificate, it creates an obligation for you to provide future meals at no charge. To handle the sale of gift certificates, create an *Other Charge* item for Gift Certificate Sales as shown in Figure 2-18. Enter **EX** as the Tax Code so it will be listed as excluded from taxable sales for sales tax reporting purposes and enter **Gift Certificates** (liability) in the account field.

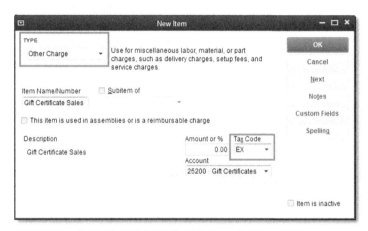

Figure 2-18 Gift Certificate Sales, Other Charge Item

For the redemption of gift certificates, create an *Other Charge* item called *Gift Certificate Redeemed*, as shown in Figure 2-19. This item will be shown as a reduction (debit) to that same account used for the sale item, **Gift Certificates** (Liability).

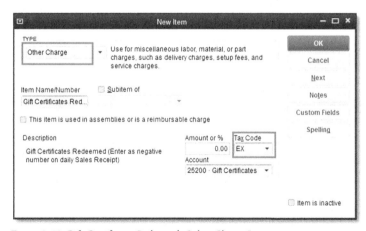

Figure 2-19 Gift Certificates Redeemed, Other Charge Item

> **Note:**
> Depending on the tax situation of the restaurant, it is possible that you will be required to treat gift certificate sales as income for income tax purposes. Check with your tax accountant or IRS regulations to be sure of the proper treatment for gift certificate sales and adjust your item setup accordingly.
>
> If you are required to treat gift certificate sales as income, we recommend you periodically record journal entries to adjust the *Gift Certificates Liability* account and offset the proper income account. Alternatively, you can enter an income account for Gift Certificate Sales and use that account in the *Gift Certificate Sales* Item and create a contra-income account for Gift Certificates Redeemed and use that account in the *Gift Certificate Redeemed* Item. If you make changes to the setup, double-check to ensure that the sales tax reports are reflecting the correct information.

Items for Tracking Tips

To track and record tips collected by credit card, you'll need to set up three *Other Charge Items* to use when you record your sales in QuickBooks.

1. Tips Collected – Credit card

2. Tips Paid

3. Tips Out Liability

As you'll see later, these *Items* will be used on a daily *Sales Receipt* for each server in the restaurant. The key function these *Items* perform is to track tips collected on credit cards and then later paid out to servers.

By using *Other Charge Items*, the amounts recorded as tips will not affect sales reports or sales tax liability reports.

> **Note:**
> *Tips Collected – Credit Card* includes tips left on credit cards and tips left on house account charges. These tips will be paid out in cash to servers at the end of their shift. House account charges are discussed later in this book.

Tips Collected – Credit Card is an *Other Charge* Item (Figure 2-20). Use **Employee Tips Payable** as the *account*, and **EX** as the *Tax Code*. This item will increase the *Employee Tips Payable* clearing account to reflect credit card and house account tips collected that need to be paid to servers in cash each night.

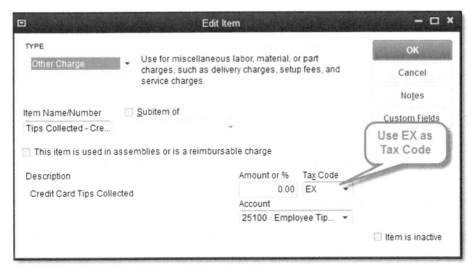

Figure 2-20 Tips Collected, Credit Card, Other Charge Item

The *Tips Paid* Item (Figure 2-21) uses **Cash on Hand** as the *account* and **EX** as the *Tax Code*. This item will reduce the *Cash on Hand* account to reflect the cash paid out in tips to servers each night. You'll see how these work later when we record sales using a QuickBooks *Sales Receipt*, starting on page 63.

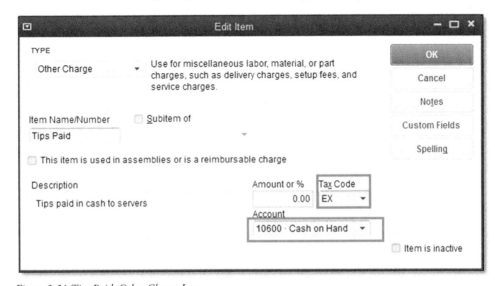

Figure 2-21 Tips Paid, Other Charge Item

The *Tips Out Liability* Item (Figure 2-22) uses **Employee Tips Payable** as
the *account* and **EX** as the *Tax Code.* This item will reduce the *Employee Tip
Payable* clearing account to reflect tips paid to servers in cash each night.

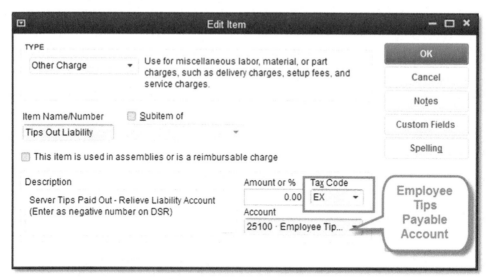

Figure 2-22 Tips Out Liability, Other Charge Item

Discounts, Loyalty Rewards, and Complimentary Items

In order to properly account for discounts and complimentary items, such as
percentage off specials, meals comp'd by a manager, or loyalty rewards
program discounts, set up one or more *Discount* items that use **Marketing
Expenses: Complimentary Food & Beverages** as the *account*, as shown in
Figure 2-23. The restaurant sample file has a master *Discount* type item called
Discounts with subitems underneath. Subitems are optional, but they can be
useful if you want to group similar items on reports.

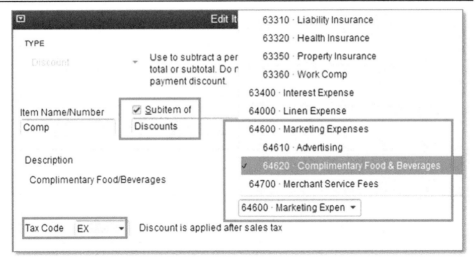

Figure 2-23 Discount Item for recording discounts and complimentary items.

The discount and complimentary items are set up with **EX** as the *Tax Code* because they are excluded from sales tax reporting.

Cash Over/Short Item

To keep track of small overages and shortages in the register, set up an *Over/Short* Item, as shown in Figure 2-24, that uses **Cash Over/Short** as the *account* and **EX** as the *Tax Code*.

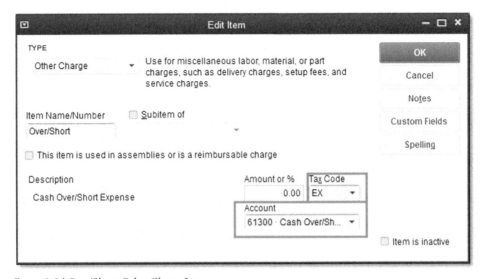

Figure 2-24 Over/Short, Other Charge Item

> **Note:**
> In our examples, we do not show any sales as non-taxable. We
> are assuming that all food and beverages that are sold are taxable
> for sales tax purposes. The rest of the items are excluded from
> sales tax reporting. If you have items that are included in total
> sales but non-taxable, such as certain takeout food or other non-
> taxable sales, be sure to set up the items to properly track the
> taxable versus non-taxable sales.

Payment Items

Payment Items are needed to represent payments received by each payment
type. When you create *Payment Items*, choose the option *Group with other
undeposited funds* for credit card payments. You will see how this works in
Chapter 7 – Bank Deposits.

Visa and MasterCard payments are generally deposited together, so you only
need one *Item* as shown in Figure 2-25. If you accept Discover Card and/or
American Express, you will generally want to create each as a separate
payment type because they are deposited separately in the bank account. The
AMEX payment method *Item* is shown in Figure 2-26.

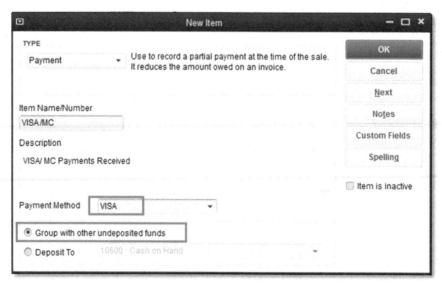

Figure 2-25 VISA/MC Payment Item to record sales paid by VISA/MC

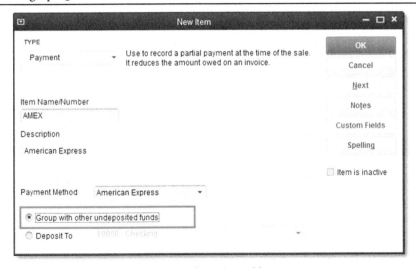

Figure 2-26 Amex Payment Item for recording sales paid by Amex

Few restaurants accept checks these days, but if you do, you have the choice of setting up one *Item* for Cash/Checks or two separate *Items*. This will depend on whether or not you are holding cash in the safe or depositing it daily along with the checks each day. If you are depositing cash daily, use the *Group with other Undeposited funds* option. If you are putting the funds in the safe, use the *Deposit to* option and select the **Cash on Hand** account. Once you understand how the *Payment Items* work, you can decide on the best setup for your particular situation.

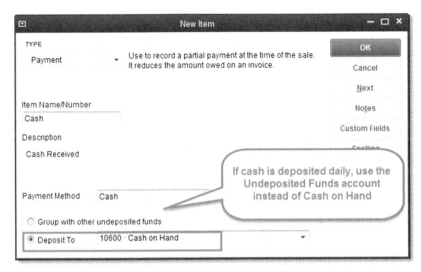

Figure 2-27 Cash Received Item to Record Sales Paid with Cash

> **Note:**
> If you are depositing cash and checks together on the same
> deposit, modify the description on the *Cash* payment item to
> *Cash/Checks Received*. There is no need to set up a separate item
> for Checks, as shown in Figure 2-28, unless you are putting the
> cash in the *Cash on Hand* account.

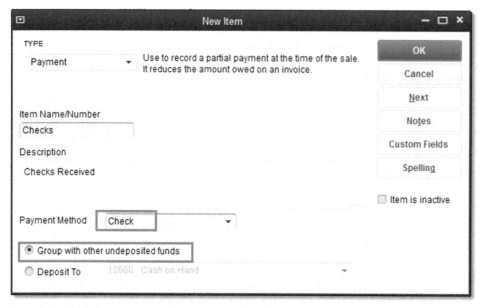

Figure 2-28 Checks Payment Item to Record Sales paid by Check

Items for Tracking House Accounts

When a customer has a house account and is allowed to put his or her food
on an account to be billed later, you will need to create two *Items* to handle
the transactions: *House Account Charges* and *House Account Invoices*. Managing
house accounts is discussed in detail in Chapter 6. For now, just set up these
Items as described below for future use.

House Account Charges shown in Figure 2-29 is an *Other Charge Item* used to
account for the fact that items were sold, but not paid for yet. Enter **House
Account Clearing** in the *account* filed. Using this *Item* will increase the *House
Account Clearing* account.

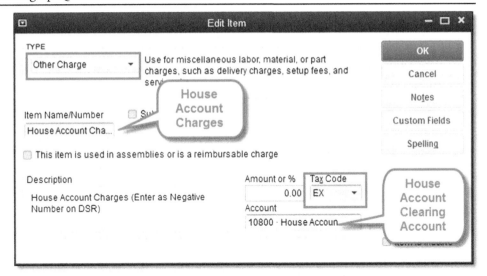

Figure 2-29 House Account Charges, Other Charge Item

House Account Invoices, shown in Figure 2-30, is an *Other Charge Item* used to record the invoices entered to the individual customer who charged his or her meals to a house account for payment at a later date. Enter **House Account Clearing** in the *account* field. Using this *Item* will decrease the *House Account Clearing* account.

When used properly on forms, these two *Items* will zero out the *House Accounts Clearing* account.

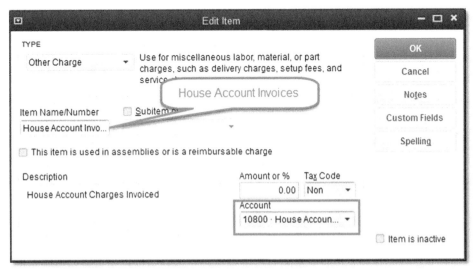

Figure 2-30 House Account Invoices, Other Charge Item

You will see how these *Items* are used in detail in the Managing House Accounts chapter.

Sales Tax Items

Sales tax is calculated by your cash register or POS system. To record the sales tax properly in QuickBooks, follow the steps on page 22 to create two new *Sales Tax Items* shown in Figure 2-31 and Figure 2-32. *CA Sales Tax* is used in the restaurant sample file. Use a name that is applicable to your restaurant. If you have multiple locations located in different sales tax jurisdictions, set up an additional *Item* for each taxing jurisdiction where tax is collected.

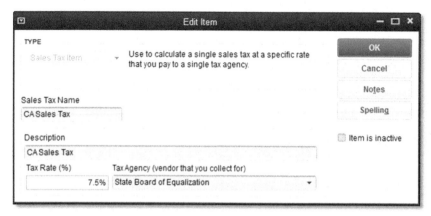

Figure 2-31 CA Sales Tax Item

The *N/A* Item is a special "dummy" Sales Tax Item that you'll use at the bottom of the daily *Sales Receipt* form.

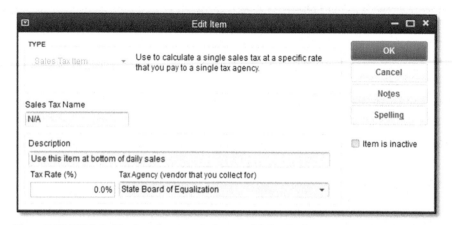

Figure 2-32 N/A Sales Tax Item for use at the bottom of daily sales forms

> **Note:**
> If your sales tax rate for a single location is remitted to more than one tax agency, you should set up separate *Sales Tax Items* for each tax agency (with the name and rate for that tax), and then create a *Sales Tax Group Item* that includes all of the component *Sales Tax Items*. Then use the group Item on your sales forms instead of the single Item we show in this example.
>
> **Note:**
> Some states require you to charge different sales tax rates for different types of sales (e.g., food is taxed at one rate, but liquor is taxed at a different rate). Make sure you set up as many *Sales Tax Items* as are needed to track the different taxes.

Using the Sales Rep List to Track Sales for Each Server

Set up a *Rep* in the *Sales Rep* list for each of your servers (or other tip-earning employees). Use *Employee* as the *Rep Type*. Employees will need to be created for each staff member. If you need more information on setting up employees, go through the complete payroll setup as discussed in our *QuickBooks Complete Textbook*, available at The Sleeter Group's online store.

If you are not using QuickBooks to process payroll, you could set up the employees in the *Other Names* list or the *Vendor* list instead of adding them to the *Employee* list. Whether you process payroll inside or outside of QuickBooks, employee names need to be added to either the *Employee* list, *Other Names* list, or *Vendor* list before you can add them to the *Sales Rep* list.

To set up Sales Reps, follow these steps:

1. Click on **Lists > Customer & Vendor Profile Lists > Sales Rep List**.

2. Select **Sales Rep** in the lower left corner and then select **New**.

3. Complete the *New Sales Rep* window as shown in Figure 2-33. The *Sales Rep Name* will be selected from the drop-down list. The initials and rep type will be filled in based on the information in the list the name was added to.

Figure 2-33 New Sales Rep

Setting up Customers and Custom Fields

For the typical restaurant setup, you'll only need to add one customer representing all customers who dine at the restaurant, as opposed to adding each of their names separately.

> **Note:**
> If you sell to customers who pay later (Accounts Receivable customers), you will also set up a separate record for each of those customers, as discussed in the Managing House Accounts chapter.

To create a new customer, follow these steps:

1. Select **Customers** from the *Home* page.

2. Create a new customer and enter *All Customers* in the *Customer Name* and *Company Name* field. You can leave all the address fields blank.

3. Then click the *Sales Tax Settings* tab on the left hand side.

4. Select **Tax** from the *Tax Code* drop-down and **N/A** from the *Tax Item* drop-down list as shown in Figure 2-34.

Figure 2-34 Customer Sales Tax Settings

5.   Click the *Additional Info* tab on the left and click **Define Fields** to set up Custom Fields for the Customer List, as shown in Figure 2-35, to help you track more information about each day's sales.

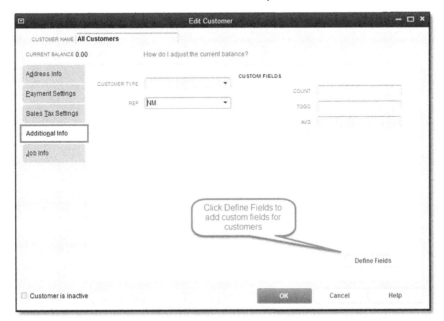

Figure 2-35 Customer Additional Info Settings

6.   Set up the Custom Fields as shown in Figure 2-36. These Custom Fields
      will be used to help you track the number of tables each waiter serves (the
      Count), how many *ToGo* orders, and the average dollar amount per
      customer. You'll see how this works later.

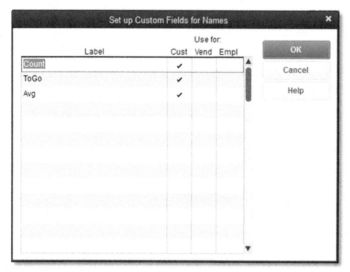

Figure 2-36 Set up Custom Fields for Names window

7.   Click **OK** twice to complete the customer record setup.

Days of Week (Shipping Method List)

In order to use the custom field *Wkday* to capture the day of the week, we
need to modify the *Shipping Method List*. This information can be added to
reports to spots trends in server sales based on the day of the week.

To modify this list, follow these steps:

1.   Click on **Lists > Customer & Vendor Profile Lists > Ship Via List**.

2.   Click on **Shipping Method** in the lower left corner and click **New**.

3.   Type *Sun* and click **Next**.

4.   Add the remaining days of the week.

5.   Click **OK** when done.

Vendor Type Code List

QuickBooks allows you to group your vendors into common types. For example, if you create a *Vendor Type* called *Beverage Supply* and you tag each of your beverage supplier vendor records with this type, a report specific to this *Vendor Type* can be created.

QuickBooks automatically creates several vendor types for you to use, including Consultant, Service Providers, Suppliers, Supplies, and Tax Agency. In addition to these default vendor types, the restaurant sample file includes vendor types for 1099 Contractor, Beverage Supply, Entertainment, Food Supply, and Insurance.

To add vendor types to your QuickBooks file, follow these steps:

1. Click on **Lists > Customer & Vendor Profile Lists > Vendor Type List**.

2. Click on **Vendor Type** in the lower left corner and click **New**.

3. Type *Entertainment* and click **Next** to enter another vendor type.

4. Click **OK** when done.

> **Note:**
> Subtypes are also allowed in the *Vendor Type List*. For example, you may want to have a vendor type called *Suppliers* with subtypes for *Food Supply, Beverage Supply, Restaurant Supply*, and so on.

Templates

In order to record your daily sales from the cash register or POS system as well as create house account invoices, you'll need to create special *Templates*. The restaurant sample file already contains the *Restaurant Daily Sales* (Sales Receipt) template and a *House Charges* (Invoice). If you want to export the templates from the restaurant sample file and import them into another company file, see page 186:

If you don't want to import the templates, follow the steps below to set up the new templates yourself.

Custom Sales Receipt Template

1. Click **Lists > Templates**.

2. From the *Templates* menu at the bottom of the list, select **New**. Then select **Sales Receipt** and click **OK**.

3. Click **Manage Templates** and enter *Restaurant Daily Sales* in the *Template Name* field on the right hand side and click **OK**.

4. The *Basic Customization* window opens.

5. Click on **Additional Customization** on the bottom of the window.

6. Edit the *Screen* and *Print* check marks and *Titles* for the *Header* and *Columns* tabs as shown in Figure 2-37 and Figure 2-38. As you uncheck the unnecessary boxes, message will pop up about Layout Designer. Click **OK**.

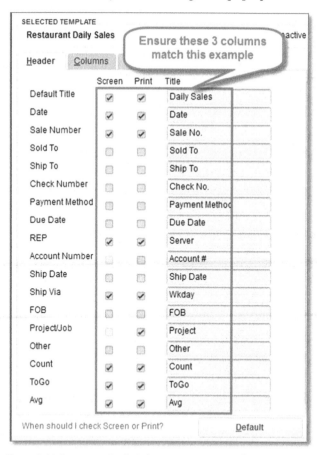

Figure 2-37 Restaurant Daily Sales Receipt Setup, Header

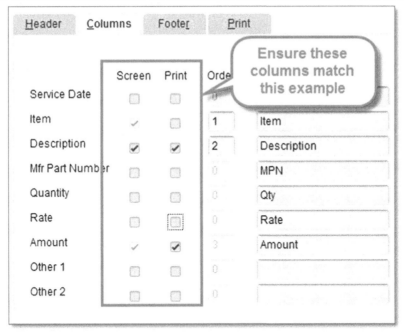

Figure 2-38 Restaurant Daily Sales Receipt Setup, Columns

7.   After you've configured all the fields in the *Sales Receipt Template*, click **OK** twice to close the template.

Custom Invoice Template

1.   Click **Lists > Templates**.

2.   From the *Templates* menu at the bottom of the list, select **New**. Then select **Invoice** and click **OK**.

3.   Click **Manage Templates** and enter ***House Charges*** in the *Template Name* field on the right side and click **OK**.

4.   The *Basic Customization* window opens.

5.   Click on **Additional Customization** on the bottom of the window.

6.   Edit the *Screen* and *Print* check marks and *Titles* for the *Header* tab as shown in Figure 2-39 and the *Columns* tabs as shown in Figure 2-40. As you uncheck the unnecessary boxes, message will pop up about Layout Designer. Click **OK**.

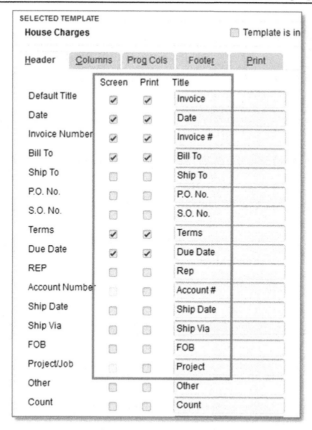

Figure 2-39 House Charges Invoice Template, Header

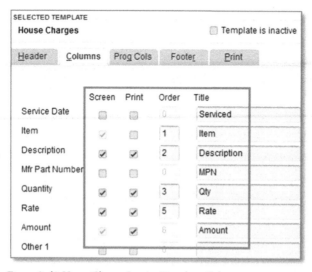

Figure 2-40 House Charges Invoice Template, Columns

Managing Templates

There are several Intuit-created templates included in the company file. You can inactivate the majority of these templates by selecting the name of each unwanted template and clicking **Templates** in the lower left corner, and then clicking **Make Template Inactive**, as shown in Figure 2-41.

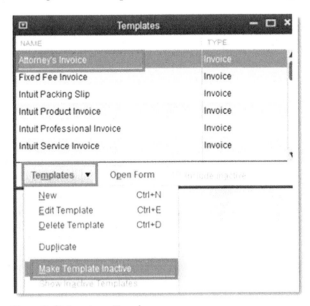

Figure 2-41 Inactivate Templates

After you have made one template inactive, you can click on **Include Inactive** box on the bottom of the list to see the inactive templates, designated by a gray "X." From this screen you can easily inactivate other templates by placing your cursor to the left of the template name. The cursor will turn into a gray "X." Simply click the invisible box to the left of the template name to inactivate each template.

To view only the active templates, uncheck the **Include Inactive** box. You will see a much shorter list of templates. You only need to have four templates as shown in Figure 2-42.

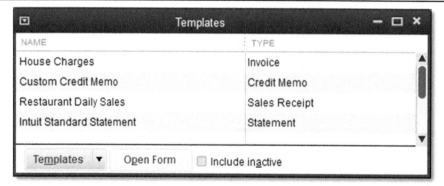

Figure 2-42 Active Templates List

Chapter 3
Tracking Tips

One of the most challenging parts of managing accounting for restaurants is the issue of "Tips." Earlier in the book, you learned how to set up *Items* for tracking tips, so this section focuses on how the accounting works for tracking tips. Later in the book you'll put together what you learned about *Items* plus what you learn here about Tips Tracking to create a simple daily routine for recording tip collections and tip payments to staff. Adding tips to paychecks is discussed starting on page 58 of Chapter 4 – Customizing Payroll for Restaurants.

> **Note:**
> For the IRS requirements relating to reporting tip income, including employee requirements, employer requirements, and reporting for allocation of tips, see the document on the IRS website titled, *Reporting Tip Income – Restaurant Tax Tips*.

Thankfully, you'll never have to directly record these debit and credit accounting entries if you use the methods described in this book. Using the tip tracking *Items* that we set up on page 26 and recording the daily sales totals from the end-of-day report (Z-tape) on a QuickBooks *Sales Receipt* as shown in the section beginning on page 63 will ensure that all of the accounting entries will be done behind the scenes for you.

Accounting for Tips

When a customer includes a tip on his/her credit card when paying their bill, the money is deposited into the restaurant's bank account. These tips are not sales of the business, they belong to the employee and need to be paid out in cash at the end of the night. The deposit of the tips into the company's bank account creates a liability for the restaurant. Using the *Tips Collected – Credit Card* Item when recording the daily sales handles the credit to the *Employee Tips Payable* account automatically.

When you pay cash tips out to each of the servers at the end of the night from the cash collected, you are paying off the liability. Using the *Tips Out Liability* Item handles the debit to the *Employee Tips Payable* account. Simultaneously, that cash that was paid is coming from the cash collected for the day. Using the *Tips Paid* Item will credit the *Cash on Hand* account.

It's a good idea to have the server sign a statement or form acknowledging receipt of her or his tips at the end of the night.

If the cash collected for the day is not enough to pay out the servers' tips, the restaurant may need to replenish the *Cash on Hand* account. To replenish the *Cash on Hand* account, write a check payable to *Cash* and take it to the bank and cash it. In QuickBooks, code this check to *Cash on Hand*.

> **Note:**
> Credit card tips include tips paid by credit card as well as tips charged to a house account. House account tips also need to be paid to the servers at the end of the night. There is no separate *Item* for House Tips. They are included with credit card tips charged.

When you get to Chapter 5 – Recording Daily Sales , the sales receipt in Figure 5-4 shows three lines where tips are recorded. The first one comes straight off of the cash register Z-tape (*Tips Collected – Credit Card*), and the other two are used to record the cash paid out (*Tips Paid)* and the reduction in the tips liability account (*Tips Out Liability)*. We do this to consolidate all of the accounting into a single sales receipt per server per day, while maintaining a trail of what transpired.

A graphic of the accounting behind the scenes for employee tips is shown in Figure 3-1.

Figure 3-1 Accounting for Tips, Behind the Scenes

Tips and Payroll

Employees need to be taxed on the tips they receive. The tips reports that
QuickBooks provides will not be sufficient for payroll reporting purposes

because the POS system is not providing information on the Z-tape regarding any cash tips picked up from the table.

It is common for servers to share their cash and credit card tips collected with the bus person, host, bartender, chef and other restaurant staff. It is ultimately each tipped employee's responsibility to keep a log of all tips collected, both in credit card tips and cash, less what was paid out to others and provide it to the restaurant so the tips can be included with payroll for tax purposes. An example of this form is shown in Figure 3-2.

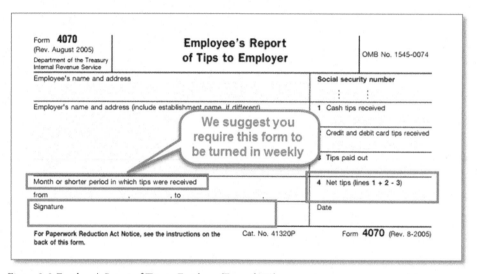

Figure 3-2 Employee's Report of Tips to Employer (Form 4070)

We recommend that you require all employees who receive tips to turn in this form, or one that is substantially similar, on a weekly basis. Tips are taxable for state and federal payroll tax purposes, but since the employee has already received the tips in cash, they are subtracted from net pay after they are taxed. We will cover how to handle payroll in Chapter 4 – Customizing Payroll for Restaurants.

> **Note:**
> IRS tax topic 761 states that when the restaurant charges a service charge to large parties or charges customers a mandated delivery service charge, these are not considered tips and need to be taxed as non-tip wages. If paid out to the employees at the end of the night, they will be treated as employee advances and will need to be tracked and deducted from payroll as an advance repayment.

> Employees need to submit a signed statement agreeing to the amount being deducted from their payroll check for all mandated service charges paid to them. This is separate from the tip reporting form shown in Figure 3-2.
>
> Additional information on this topic can be found in this IRS article, Tips versus service charges: How to report.

Employer Tax Credits

You should check with your tax advisor to see if your restaurant is eligible for the *Credit for Employer on Social Security and Medicare Taxes Paid on Certain Employee Tips* (IRS Form 8846). The form and instructions can be found on the IRS website at http://www.irs.gov/pub/irs-access/f8846_accessible.pdf.

QuickBooks provides a Form 8846 worksheet to use to gather information needed to compute the credit. The report is found under **Reports > Employees & Payroll > Summarize payroll data in excel**. Once you run this report, there will be a tab on the worksheet called **8846**. Check with your tax advisor and double-check the information exported for accuracy before filing Form 8846.

Chapter 4
Customizing Payroll for Restaurants

QuickBooks Payroll (Basic, Enhanced, Assisted, or Online Payroll) is very well suited for most of the needs of small restaurants with fewer than 50 employees. In this section, we will discuss how to set up QuickBooks internal payroll (Basic, Enhanced, or Assisted) as it relates to restaurants.

We expect that you are already familiar with the basic functionality of QuickBooks Payroll features, including setting up *Payroll Items* and adding employees. If you need more information on setting up payroll, go through the payroll setup chapter in our *QuickBooks Complete Textbook,* available at The Sleeter Group's online store.

If you don't plan to use QuickBooks to calculate your payroll, you will still need to ensure that employees are submitting IRS Form 4070 (see Figure 3-2) or something similar so you can determine the amount of tips collected and report them to your outside payroll service. If you are using an outside payroll service, be sure to add your employee names to the *Vendor* list or *Other Names* list so that you can set them up in the *Sales Reps* list, which facilitates the separate tracking of sales for each server.

Wage Payroll Items

Wage Items can be customized to keep track of costs by staffing position. Perhaps the restaurant owner wants to know how much he or she paid to bartenders, cooks, host, chefs, dishwashers, and servers. This can be tracked by using *Wage Items* in the *Payroll Items* list.

The following *Payroll Items* are examples of some wage items you could create:

Chef	Bus Person
Cook	Manager
Server	Host Person

Each of these could be set up as hourly or salary *Payroll Items* depending on each restaurant's particular needs. It is possible to have several *Payroll Items* for each position. For example, you may have Chef-Salary, Chef-Hourly, and Chef-Overtime. Though we will not discuss the setup of *Wage Items* in detail, be sure to include *Payroll Items* for regular hourly pay, overtime pay, sick pay, and vacation pay as applicable – and assign them to the employees in the *Employee Center*. You can choose whether to post all of the *Items* to one account for gross wages, or you can set up separate accounts in the *Chart of Accounts* to separate them out based on your own criteria (manager wages, bar wages, kitchen wages, server wages, etc.).

The *Payroll Items* can be viewed by selecting the *Lists* menu, then choosing *Payroll Item List*. From here you can add or edit *Payroll Items*.

To view the total wages paid by staff position, click on **Reports > Employees & Payroll > Payroll Summary**.

Tips Payroll Items

Two payroll items, *Tips Addition* and *Tips Deduction*, are needed so the employee can be taxed on his or her tips, which have already been paid to them in cash. Using these items is discussed later in this chapter beginning on page 58.

To create the *Payroll Item* called **Tips Addition**, follow these steps:

1. Click on **Lists > Payroll Item List**.

2. Click **Ctrl+N** to add a new payroll item.

3. Select the *Custom Setup* option as shown in Figure 4-1 and click **Next**.

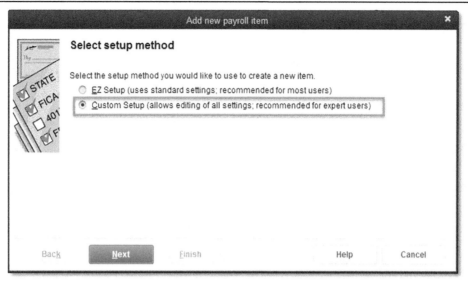

Figure 4-1 Add New Payroll Item, Custom Setup

4. Select the **Addition** radio button and click **Next**.

5. Enter *Tips Addition* in the name field and click **Next**.

6. Assign the *Account* to **Gross Wages**. The account that you choose will be used as a clearing account of sorts. The amount added with this item will be deducted out with the *Tips Deduction* item.

> **Note:**
> If you prefer, set up a separate expense account to track tips collected and paid and call it **Tips Clearing** to use for the *Tips Addition* and *Tips Deduction* payroll items.

7. Assign the *Tax Tracking Type* to **Reported Tips** as shown in Figure 4-2 and click **Next**. This will ensure that the tips are reported in the correct box on the employees' IRS Form W-2s.

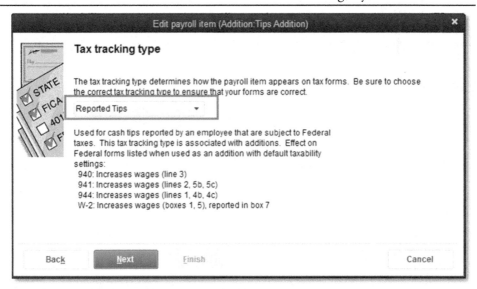

Figure 4-2 Tips Addition Payroll Item, Tax Tracking Type

8.   Accept the default tax settings shown on the *Taxes* screen and click **Next**.

9.   Accept **Neither** as the *Calculate based on quantity* window and click **Next**.

10.   The Default rate and limit are left alone.

11.   Complete the item setup by clicking **Finish**.

To create the *Payroll Item* called **Tips Deduction**, follow these steps:

1.   Select **Lists > Payroll Item List**.

2.   Click **Ctrl+N** to add a new payroll item.

3.   Select the *Custom Setup* option as shown in Figure 4-1 and click **Next**.

4.   Select the **Deduction** radio button and click **Next**.

5.   Enter *Tips Deduction* in the name field and click **Next**.

6.   Leave the agency name and number fields blank, and assign the *Liability Account* to **Gross Wages**. This will offset the *Tips Addition* item and result in a zero net amount posting to this account. Click **Next**.

7.   Assign the *Tax Tracking Type* to **None** as shown in Figure 4-3 and click **Next**.

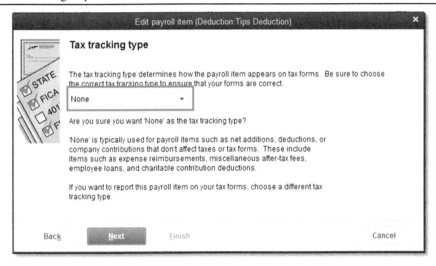

Figure 4-3 Tips Deduction Payroll Item, Tax Tracking Type

8. Accept the default tax settings on the *Taxes* screen and click **Next**.

9. Accept **Neither** as the *Calculate based on quantity* window and click **Next**.

10. On the *Gross vs. net* window (Figure 4-4), choose **Net pay** and click **Next**.

Figure 4-4 Tips Deduction Payroll Item, Gross vs. Net

11. The Default rate and limit are left alone.

12. Complete the item setup by clicking **Finish**.

Setting up Employees

Set up your employees as you normally would in the *Employee Center*.

If you plan to track hours for employees and pay them based on hours worked, mark the *Use Time Data to Create Paychecks* field on each employee record in the *Payroll Info* screen, as shown in Figure 4-5.

Add the *Tips Addition* and *Tips Deduction* payroll items to all tipped employees.

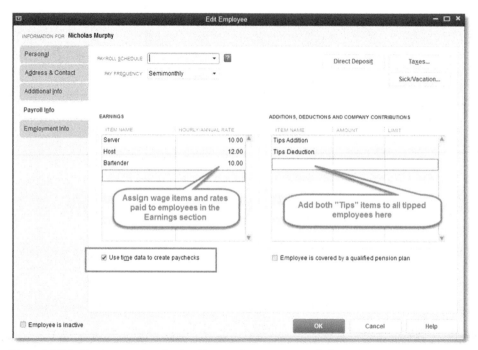

Figure 4-5 Edit Employee window showing Use time data to create paychecks

The rest of the employee setup remains that same as it would for any other QuickBooks payroll setup.

Tracking Time in QuickBooks

Many POS systems will allow employees to track their time and generate a report that can be used to pay the employees. If you are using your POS system to track time, be sure it complies with all state regulations and disregard the rest of this subsection.

To use QuickBooks to track time, record the activities performed by each employee during a one-week period on the *Weekly Timesheet*, following these steps:

1. From the *Home* Page, click on **Enter Time** and select **Use Weekly Timesheet**.

2. Enter the employee name in the *Name* field.

3. Use the **Previous** arrow at the top of the screen to find the correct date range.

4. The *Customer* and *Service Item* columns are left blank.

5. Enter the *Payroll Item* that will be used on the paychecks (Server-Hourly, Chef-Hourly, Host-Overtime, etc.).

6. For each day, enter in the total number of hours worked for this employee, as shown in Figure 4-6.

Figure 4-6 Weekly Timesheet

> **Note:**
> Depending on the preferences you chose in Figure 2-5 on page 11, you will either enter 6.5 or 6:30 for six hours and thirty minutes.

7. Ensure that the box *Billable* is unchecked.

> **Tip:**
> Use the *Time & Expenses* Company Preferences as discussed on page 14 to make the billable box default to unchecked and to set the first day of your workweek.

8. Click on **Save & New** or **Save & Close** when you have entered all of the time for this employee.

> **Tip:**
> There are several third party programs that will allow your employees to track time on their smartphones or other Internet-connected devices that will allow for manager approval processes. Time can be automatically imported into QuickBooks timesheets for payroll preparation. For more information on time tracking products that integrate with QuickBooks, visit https://apps.intuit.com/

Adding Tips to Employee Paychecks

Whether you use QuickBooks to process payroll or an outside service provider, you'll need to add tips onto each employee's paycheck so she or he can pay taxes on them. Since the employee has already received the tips in cash, you will also back this amount out. Employees will need to complete, date, and sign IRS Form 4070 or something similar, as shown in Figure 3-2, so you know the amount of tips to include on the payroll checks.

Once you know how much money each employee received in tips from all sources, report them to the outside payroll provider or follow these steps to add and subtract the tips from the paychecks in QuickBooks:

1. Click on **Employees > Pay Employees** to open the *Payroll Center*.

2. Click on **Start Unscheduled Payroll** or **Start Scheduled Payroll** depending on whether or not you are using the payroll schedule functionality. For more information on payroll schedules, click on **Help** inside QuickBooks.

3. The *Enter Payroll Information* window will open.

4. If you have set up the employees to use time data to create paychecks, as discussed earlier in this chapter, a list of employees to pay will populate with their hours from the *Weekly Timesheet*.

5. Confirm that the hours shown are correct and click **Continue**.

6. Confirm that the correct *pay period end* date and *check date* are shown.

7. Choose the correct bank account to create payroll checks.

8. Click on **Open Paycheck Detail** as shown in Figure 4-7 to enter the tip information.

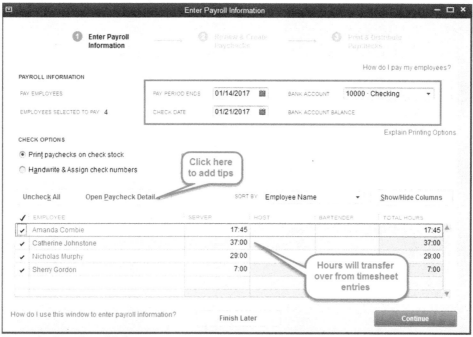

Figure 4-7 Enter Payroll Information

9. In the *Other Payroll Items* section, add the amount of tips paid using the *Tips Addition* payroll item and subtract the same amount using the *Tips Deduction* payroll item as shown in Figure 4-8. Setting up and using these tips items properly ensures that payroll taxes are calculated and paid on the tips previously received by the employee and that the tips paid will be reported correctly on W-2 forms

10. Continue processing payroll as you normally would.

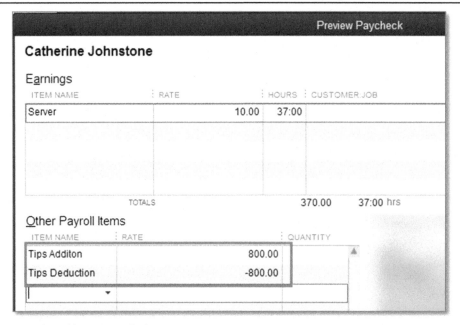

Figure 4-8 Add Tips to Paychecks

Handling Negative Paychecks

An employee's regular paycheck (that includes his or her *Tips Addition/Deduction*) may not provide enough in non-tip wages to cover the payroll taxes due on the wages and tips. This creates a negative paycheck, which you cannot process.

When this happens, you must rely on the IRS ordering rules to handle this issue. As of the date of this publication, the guidelines are found in Tax Topic 761. This is an excerpt from the IRS website:

If you don't have enough money from the employee's wages ... withhold taxes in the following order:

- *Social Security and Medicare taxes on the employee's wages,*

- *Federal income taxes on the employee's wages,*

- *State and local taxes imposed on the employee's wages,*

- *Social Security and Medicare taxes on the employee's reported tips, and*

- *Federal income taxes on the employee's reported tips.*

The IRS is very specific regarding how to handle and report payroll taxes that are not able to be collected. To some extent, you can modify the employee payroll taxes withheld by overriding amounts on the employee summary on the paycheck detail. It gets tricky when you are not able to collect Social Security and Medicare taxes. If you are unable to easily handle the negative paycheck scenario inside QuickBooks, we recommend outsourcing payroll to a full service payroll provider who can handle the reporting for you.

Chapter 5
Recording Daily Sales

Finally! At long last, you're all set up and ready for the fun part. All of the setup we've done to this point was aimed at allowing the restaurant manager or bookkeeper to enter a single entry into QuickBooks for each server every day. That's all, just one single transaction per server per day! If you don't want to have the details of sales by server, you can modify the setup to not show sales reps but instead include one entry for the entire day for all servers. For the purposes of this chapter and future chapters, we will assume you want to see sales broken down by server.

Zeroing Out the Cash Register

Each day, at the end of business, the server or manager will "zero out" the cash register or POS system and create the reports of the day's sales. A "Z-tape" or end-of-day report, similar to the one shown in Figure 5-1, will be needed to create a single entry into QuickBooks for each server to record his or her total sales for the day.

```
Academy Restaurant
Date: 1/8/2017

Server – CJ
In: 16:30 Out: 21:30 – 5 hours
Table Count: 25
To Go: 0
Avg Ticket: 48.03

Sales Totals
Food Sales                      840.53
Bar Sales                       360.23
Gift Certificates Sold          100.00
Sales Tax                        90.06
Grand Total Sales-Incl Tax    1,390.82
Net Taxed Sales               1,200.76
Tips Collected                  144.09
Grand Total + Tips            1,534.91

Breakdown by Payment Type
Cash                            325.05
VISA/MC                         846.95
AMEX                            188.45
On Account                       57.95
Comps                            48.50
Gift Certificates Redeemed       25.00
Paid Outs                        42.00
```

Figure 5-1 Z-tape for Catherine Johnstone, Jan. 8

Entering Daily Sales by Server

The daily *Sales Receipt* entry in QuickBooks is critical to keeping proper accounting records and driving the reports described later in this book.

To record the daily sales, follow these steps to enter a different sales receipt for the total sales for each server, each day:

1.   From the *Customers* menu, select **Enter Sales Receipt**. Alternatively, you can click on **Create Sales Receipt** from the *Home* page.

2.   Enter *All Customers* in the *Customer name* field.

3.   Choose the **Restaurant Daily Sales** template.

4.   Enter the date, server's initials, weekday, total count (number of guests), the number of to go orders (if desired), and the average ticket in the top section of the form. The *Sale No.* will automatically be created based on the next

sequential number. This is merely a reference number, there is no need to change it.

5. Enter the total sales for each *Service* item (**Food sales** and **Bar sales***)* and enter a **Subtotal.**

> **Note:**
> The placement of the subtotal is crucial for creating sales tax reports. Be sure to enter it after all of your sales items and before the sales tax line.

6. On the line under the subtotal, enter the sales tax item(s) and the amount collected (per the Z-tape).

7. Enter the amount of Discounts and Gift Certificate Sales.

For the credit card tips collected shown on the Z-tape, enter three lines: **Tips Collected - Credit Card** (positive number which increases the *Employee Tips Payable* account), **Tips Paid** (positive number which reduces the *Cash on Hand* bank account) and **Tips Out Liability** (negative number that reduces the *Employee Tips Payable* liability account).

Figure 5-2 shows the accounting behind the scenes for the *Tips Collected - Credit Card* and *Tips Out Liability Items* on the employee tips payable account.

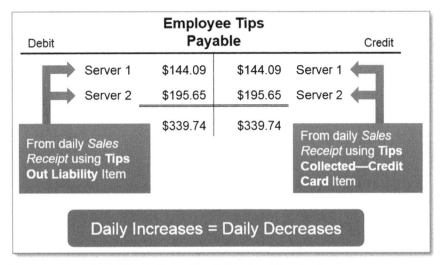

Figure 5-2 Accounting Behind the Scenes, Tips Collected and Tips Out Items

The accounting behind the scenes for the *Tips Paid* item is shown in Figure 5-3.

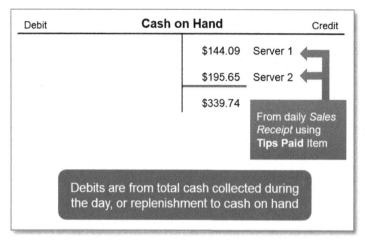

Figure 5-3 Accounting Behind the Scenes, Tips Paid Item

8. Enter the amount (as a negative number) of **House Account Charges** and **Gift Certificates Redeemed**, if any. House accounts are discussed in more detail beginning on page 71.

9. Enter each of the payment types including cash and each type of credit card (VISA/MC, Amex, etc.).

10. Enter any amounts paid out of the register that would reduce the amount of money that was collected as **Paid Outs Clearing**. The actual expenses by category will be posted as described on page 105.

11. Use the **Over/Short** item with whatever amount is needed to zero out the total at the bottom of the sales receipt. This should be a small amount. If you are off more than a few dollars, you need to scrutinize the numbers to detect errors in the POS system or potential theft. If the amount is positive, the cash drawer is over by that amount.

12. Ensure that the total at the bottom of the form is 0.00.

Notice in Figure 5-4 that sales tax is entered directly on the face of the sales receipt, and the Tax field at the bottom is set to **N/A**. This is important for properly tracking sales tax reports and making sure that the exact sales tax collected by the POS system is recorded into QuickBooks.

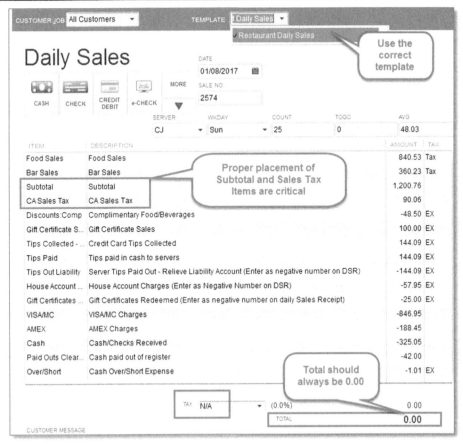

Figure 5-4 Daily Sales Receipt by Server Using Z-Tape Totals

Continue entering sales receipts for each of the servers for the day. The restaurant sample file has sales receipts for two weeks in January 2017.

The accounting behind the scenes for the daily *Sales Receipt* is shown in Figure 5-5.

Account	Item	Debit	Credit
	ASSETS		
Cash on Hand	Cash	325.05	
Cash on Hand	Tips Paid		144.09
Paid Outs Clearing	Paid Outs Clearing	42.00	
Undeposited Funds	VISA/MC	846.95	
Undeposited Funds	AMEX	188.45	
House Accounts Clearing	House Account Charges	57.95	
	LIABILITIES		
Sales Tax Payable	CA Sales Tax		90.06
Employee Tips Payble	Tips Out	144.09	
Employee Tips Payble	Tips Collected -CC		144.09
Gift Certificates Liability	Gift Cert Sales		100.00
Gift Certificates Liability	Gift Certs Redeemed	25.00	
	INCOME & EXPENSES		
Food Sales Income	Food Sales		840.53
Bar Sales Income	Bar Sales		360.23
Marketing Expenses	Discounts:Comp	48.50	
Over/Short	Over/Short	1.01	
	Totals	1,679.00	1,679.00

Figure 5-5 Accounting for Daily Sales Receipt, Behind the Scenes

The daily *Sales Receipt* is only the first step. There are other transactions to post in order to clear out the clearing accounts and undeposited funds.

Chapter 6 – Managing House Accounts, discusses how to move the balance from *House Accounts Clearing* to *Accounts Receivable* using invoices.

Chapter 7 – Bank Deposits, discusses how to move the balance from *Undeposited Funds* to the *Checking* account using the bank deposit feature.

Chapter 8 – Managing Expenses, discusses moving the expenses paid in cash out of the register from the *Paid Outs Clearing* account to the actual expense account the payment was for.

Memorized Sales Receipts

Memorized transactions allow you to efficiently enter frequent transactions. Since you'll be entering the same basic information each day, but with different amounts and server information, you could speed up your data entry by memorizing the information on the daily *Sales Receipt.*

To memorize a *Sales Receipt*, leave the *Server, Wkday, Count, ToGo* and *Avg* fields blank and add lines for all of the *Items* that you could possibly need, including a properly placed subtotal, leaving the amount column blank. Select **Memorize** at the top of the form as shown in Figure 5-6.

Figure 5-6 Memorize Sales Receipt

Give the transaction a name such as **'Daily Sales Receipt'** that you'll recognize the next time you need to enter a similar transaction. Select the radio button for **Do Not Remind Me** as shown in Figure 5-7.

Figure 5-7 Add Memorized Transaction

To use a memorized transaction as template for a new transaction, follow these steps:

1.   Display the memorized transaction list by clicking **Lists > Memorized Transaction List.**

2.   Double-click on the transaction in the list to open a new transaction.

3.   Enter the correct *date, server, wkday, count, togo* and *avg* information on the top of the form.

4.   Add the numbers for each of the line items based on the Z-tape information.

5.   Delete any unused lines by right clicking on the line and selecting **Delete Line**. This ensures that averages calculated on reports are not skewed by the quantity of entries being misstated.

6.   Confirm that the total is 0.00 and click **Save & Close**.

7.   Use the *Memorized Report List* to enter information for the rest of the servers.

> **Tip:**
> Instead of using *Memorized Transactions* to record the default *Items* used on the daily *Sales Receipt*, use a *Group* item instead. This will accomplish the same goal of not remembering every line item needed in the correct order. You can set up a *Group* item in the *Items List* by selecting **Group** as the *Item Type* and entering in all of the necessary *Items* in the correct order, including the subtotal.

Chapter 6 Managing House Accounts

Handling Accounts Receivable in Restaurants

Many restaurants have preferred customers who have the privilege of not paying for every meal at the time of service and are instead given a "house account" to charge the meals to. Also, some restaurants also provide catering services on account for repeat customers. Once a week or once a month, the restaurant will send customer statements detailing the charges on each customer's account. Customers then send payment for the total amount of the charges. Accounting for this can be a little tricky, but this section walks you through the steps necessary to account for these transactions.

In order to manage the house accounts and ensure that the customers are charged for all of their meals, two items are created *(House Account Charges* and *House Account Invoices)* to track the house account transactions. Both of these items will post to the *House Accounts Clearing* account. The setup of these items is discussed in Chapter 2 – Setting up QuickBooks for Restaurants, on page 32.

The proper use of the house account items on the daily *Sales Receipt and Invoices* will ensure that the *House Account Clearing* account shows a zero balance at the end of each day. This also allows the restaurant to send statements from QuickBooks at the end of the week or month that detail the charges made by the customer.

Daily Sales Receipt Entries

In the POS system, a new payment method should be created for "house accounts" or "on account" or another descriptive name that servers will use to show that the customer did not pay for his or her meal with cash or credit card. The total sales for the house account customers are included in the Z-tape for the day. These on account meals need to be accounted for or the server will end up short. These signed charge slips need to be turned in by each server at the end of his or her shift so the bookkeeper can create an *Invoice* for each house charge at the end of the day.

When recording the daily sales entry, use the *House Account Charges* item to record the amount of the meals that were charged, as shown in Figure 5-4 on page 67.

This *House Account Charges* Item posts the amount entered as an increase to the *House Accounts Clearing* account. The accounting behind the scenes for house account transactions is shown in Figure 6-1.

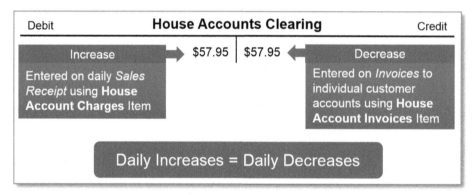

Figure 6-1 Accounting for House Accounts, Behind the Scenes

Adding House Account Customers

In order to create invoices and clear out the *House Accounts Clearing* account, you will first need to set up your customer records.

Follow these steps to set up each customer with house account privileges:

1. Open the *Customer Center* by clicking on **Customers** from the *Icon bar*.

2. Select **New Customer** from the *New Customer & Job* drop-down menu as shown in Figure 6-2.

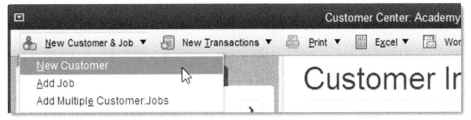

Figure 6-2 Adding a new Customer Record

3. Enter in the Customer Name as you want it to appear in your Customer Center. The list will be sorted alphabetically, so in the case of individuals you need to decide whether to use Last name, First name or First name, Last name.

4. Leave the *Opening Balance* field blank as shown in Figure 6-3.

5. Enter in the customer's address and contact information on the *Address Info* tab.

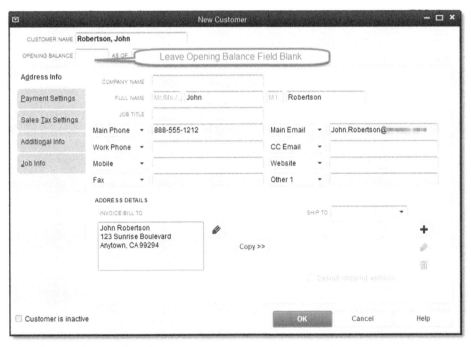

Figure 6-3 New Customer Record

6. Complete the settings on the *Payment Settings* tab, including the credit limit if desired.

7. The *Sales Tax Settings* should reflect **Tax** as the *Tax Code and* **N/A** as the *Tax Item*.

8. The *Additional Info* and *Job Info* tabs can be left as they are.

9. Click **OK** when done entering the customer information.

Creating Invoices

Creating *Invoices* for each house account charge will clear out the *House Accounts Clearing* account as shown in Figure 6-1. By creating *Invoices*, you are shifting the balance to the *Accounts Receivable* account where you can run reports and send periodic statements to customers.

In order to create the invoices, you will need to know the name of the customer, date, and amount of the transaction. In order to provide the customer with proof of the authorized charges, copies of the charge slips with the customer's signature turned in as part of the daily paperwork should be sent to the customer.

> **Note:**
> Consider scanning these signed charge receipts and saving them electronically so you can include them with the customer statement.

To create the *Invoices*, follow these steps:

1. Click on the **Create Invoices** icon on the *Home page* and enter in the name of customer.

> **Did You Know?**
> When you type the first few characters of any field that has a list behind it, QuickBooks completes the field using a feature called *QuickFill*. QuickFill uses the first few characters you type to find the name in the list. If the name does not come up right away, keep typing until the correct name appears.

2. Choose the **House Charges** template that was created on page 41.

3. Enter in the *Date* of the charged meal and press **Tab.**

> **Note:**
> The first time you enter an *Invoice*, enter any number you want
> in the *Invoice #* field. QuickBooks will automatically number
> future *Invoices* incrementally. You can change or reset the
> numbering at any time by overriding the number on a future
> *Invoice*.

4.   Press **Tab** to accept the default *Invoice #*.

5.   Press **Tab** again to accept the *Bill To* information.

6.   Enter in the *Terms* for this charge, which populates the *Due Date*.

Based on the time frame within which you expect the customer to pay this
invoice, you can enter in a particular due date in the *Due Date* field rather than
using standard terms. For example, the restaurant may send out statements on the
1st of the month and expect payment to be made on the 10th of the following
month. In the example in Figure 6-4, we expect to send the statement on
February 1, so payment will be due on February 10.

7.   Press **Tab** or use your mouse to click on the *Item* field.

8.   Enter in **House Account Invoices** in the *Item* field. This item offsets the
        amounts you entered on the daily *Sales Receipt* and clears out the *House
        Account Clearing* account.

9.   Enter one invoice for each house charge. Confirm that the balance in the
        House Accounts Clearing account is zero by opening the register or running a
        transaction detail report.

10.   Completed invoices will look like Figure 6-4.

> **Note:**
> Alternatively, you can enter the house charges using the
> *Statement Charges* feature in the *Customers* menu. For more
> information, press **F1** and search for **Enter charges for billing
> statements**. Entering statement charges will create invoice
> transactions automatically.

The amounts posted from the daily *Sales Receipts* and the amount of *Invoices*
entered for the individual house charge will cancel each other out, resulting in
a zero balance in the *House Clearing* account.

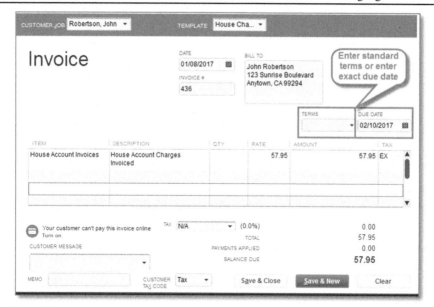

Figure 6-4 House Account Invoice

You can choose to mark the invoices to print later. An alternative to printing and mailing – or emailing – each individual invoice is to create and send a *Statement* along with the copies of the authorized charge slips turned in by the servers to the customer each week or at the end of the month, depending on the volume of transactions.

> **Note:**
> QuickBooks allows for printing or emailing of invoices and statements. You can set up the *Preferred Delivery Method* in the *Payment Settings* tab in the customer record.

House Account Reports

Now that you've entered *Invoices* for your customers, QuickBooks provides you with reports that reflect the balances owed by your customers.

Open Invoices Report

The *Open Invoices* displays all of the unpaid invoices by customer. The age of each transaction is based on the aging preference, as discussed under *Reports & Graphs – Company Preferences* on page 12.

To create the *Open Invoices* report (Figure 6-5), follow these steps:

1. Click on **Reports > Customers & Receivables > Open Invoices**.

2. The default *Dates* setting is **All**. You can change the date at the top of the report to today, the end of the previous month, or the end of the previous week based on what time frame you want to review.

3. The *Aging* column in the example is blank since these invoices are not past due.

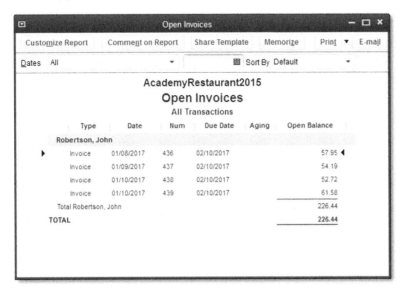

Figure 6-5 Open Invoices Report

Aging Summary Report

To see which customers have the oldest unpaid balances, you can run an **Aging Summary** report. This report lists the customers and their balances based on the criteria you select, and groups them according to how long they are past due.

To create the *Aging Summary* report (Figure 6-6), follow these steps:

1. Click **Reports > Customers & Receivables > A/R Aging Summary**.

2. Set the **Dates** filed at the top of the report to today, the end of the previous month, or the end of the previous week based on what time frame you want to review.

3.   The report will default to 30 day increments for each column with a
       maximum of 90 days. You can choose to change the interval to weekly by
       entering **7** in the *Interval (days)* filed and **45** in the *Through (days past due)*
       field.

The invoices for *John Robertson* shown in Figure 6-6 are listed as current
because they are not yet past due. If there were any past due invoices, they
would be shown in the appropriate column.

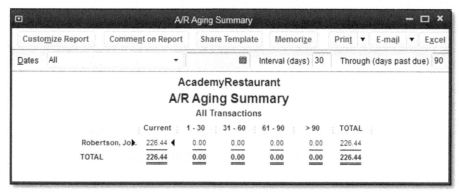

Figure 6-6 Accounts Receivable Aging Summary

It's important to run these reports and review them regularly to ensure that
customers are paying their bills in a timely manner. It may be necessary to
suspend house account charging privileges if customers are not paying their
bills on a regular basis.

Statements

QuickBooks Customer *Statements* provide a summary of the individual
charges that were charged on the house account. Statements should be sent
out every 30 days or sooner. You may want to send them out each week for
customers who have a high volume of house charges. This will help ensure
that the restaurant gets paid in a timely manner.

In order to create statements, follow these steps:

1.   From the *Home* page, click the **Statements** icon to open the *Create
       Statements* window as shown in Figure 6-7.

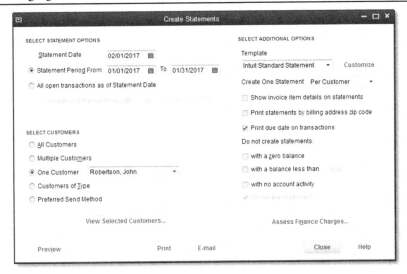

Figure 6-7 Create Statements window

2.   In the *Select Statement Options* section, enter in the desired statement date in the *Statement Date* field. This will usually be the first day of the week following the charges or the first day of the following month.

3.   There are two choices for the type of statement to create. You can either show all of the transactions for a given period of time, or you can choose to show only the open transactions.

      The *Statement period* option will show the beginning balance along with the charges and payments made for the selected period and the total amount owed.

      The *All open transactions* option will show each charge that was not paid. This is an individual preference and you will need to choose the option that works best for you.

4.   To create a *Statement period* type of Customer *Statement,* click the radio button next to this option and set the *Statement Period From* and *To* fields for the desired week or month.

5.   To create the *All open transactions* type of Customer *Statement,* click the radio button next to this option.

6.   In the *Select Customers* section, you can choose to create statements for all customers, multiple customers, one customer, or customers of a certain type.

Note:
If some customers get their statements weekly and others get them monthly, you can add a customer type in the *Additional Info* tab of the Customer record and use it to filter which statements are created. Customer types can be created using the same steps used to add vendor types discussed on page 39 by opening the *Customer Type List*.

---

7.   In the *Select Additional Options* section, you can select whether or not to show the invoice line item descriptions on the statements as well as additional criteria for which customers to create statements for. Experiment with these settings to discover the format that works best for the restaurant.

8.   Click on **Preview** to view the statements (Figure 6-8) before printing to ensure that the format is correct.

9.   Next, choose to **Print** or **Email** *Statements* to the customers. If you have entered an email address into the *Customer* record, QuickBooks will allow you to send the statements electronically.

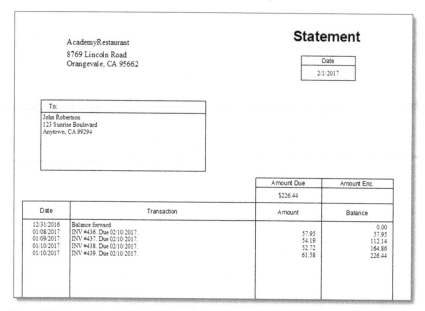

Figure 6-8 John Robertson Monthly Statement

We recommended that you print the statements and mail them to the customer with copies of the signed charge slips. Depending on the relationship between the customer and the restaurant, this may not be necessary, but you will need to have those charge slips available in the event of a dispute.

> **Tip:**
> You can customize your statements to include your company logo and change the style and layout using the layout designer. For more information on customizing forms, press **F1** inside QuickBooks and search for **Logo**. You can also search **Customize your forms** for an overview and links to additional resources.

Receiving Payments

When the customer sends in payment for his or her house account charges, the payment needs to be posted against the invoice so the next statement sent to the customer properly reflects the payment and reduces his or her account balance.

To record payments received from your customer and apply the payment to specific *Invoices*, follow these steps:

1. Click **Receive Payments** on the *Home* page to open the *Receive Payments* window.

2. Select **Robertson, John** in the *Received From* field.

> **Note:**
> Once a customer is selected, the *Customer Payment* window shows the open Invoices for that specific customer. This section shows the dates of each of the invoices that were created based on the house charges, along with the invoice number, original amount, and the amount due.

3. Enter the amount of the payment in the *Amount* field and then press **Tab**.

4. Enter the date of the payment in the *Date* field and then press **Tab**.

5. Select the **Check** icon as the payment method and then press **Tab**.

6. Enter the check number in the *Reference #* field and then press **Tab**.

7.   QuickBooks will automatically apply the amount received to the oldest invoices as long as you have set your preferences as described on page 11.

8.   To change the invoices automatically applied, check or uncheck the column to the left of the invoice date.

9.   Verify that the **Amount Due** and amount **Applied** match as shown in Figure 6-9.

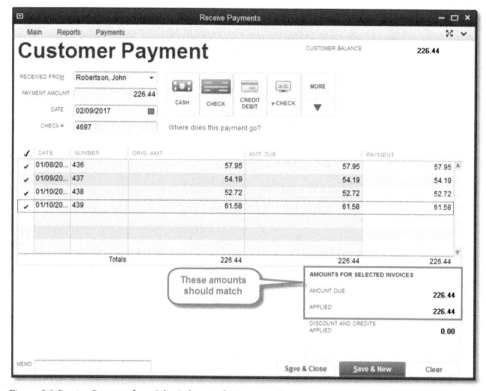

Figure 6-9 Receive Payment from John Robertson for January Charges

10. QuickBooks will automatically group this payment with other undeposited funds to be deposited with other funds collected as described in the next chapter.

Chapter 7
Bank Deposits

After recording the daily sales receipts for each server, the *Undeposited Funds* account has a balance that includes the individual cash and credit card payment items that were entered on each of the servers' daily *Sales Receipts*. The total credit card payments for all servers for the day will post to the bank account as one deposit. These amounts, as well as cash and checks deposited, must be grouped together and transferred into the bank account so that the bank reconciliation will match with each day's transactions.

Depositing Credit Card Receipts

As part of the daily closing process, the restaurant manager will "batch out" the credit card terminal and a batch report will be printed and included with the daily paperwork. This batch report includes the total credit card payments collected by all of the servers for the entire day.

> Tip:
> Ask the credit card processing company to provide online access to the merchant account so you can see batch reports online and avoid the need to for the manager to print them at the end of each day.

You can do this daily or wait until the deposits actually show up at the bank. By recording the deposits daily, you will know exactly how much money should be hitting the bank and you may locate errors that may have happened in the funding process. Although they are rare, errors are sometimes made by credit card companies.

In order for your bank account reconciliation to go smoothly, you will need to group the deposits for the day by payment type. VISA/MC for the day will be put on one deposit, Discover on another, and American Express on another.

> **Note:**
> Merchant processing systems will often be configured to automatically batch out at a particular time of day. If the restaurant's merchant account is configured to automatically close batches each day, we recommend that you schedule this to happen during off hours (e.g., at 4:00 a.m.). This will ensure that the amount of credit card deposits posted from the Z-tape totals will match the bank deposit from the merchant processor.

To record the deposit of credit card receipts, follow these steps:

1. Click on **Banking > Make Deposit**. The *Payments to Deposit* screen will show all of the payment details that you entered on the *Sales Receipts*.

2. Click on *Sort payments by* to select **Payment Method**, as shown in Figure 7-1, to make it easier to group the payments.

3. Select all of the lines for VISA payments for a single day to group them together onto a single deposit and click **OK**. The *Make Deposits* window will open showing a summary of the payments being grouped together, as show in Figure 7-2.

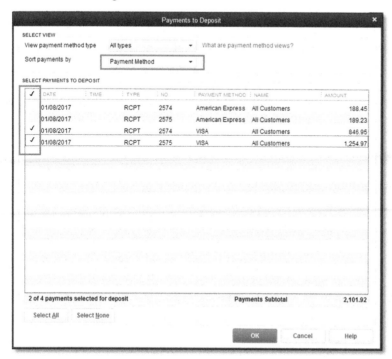

Figure 7-1 Payments to Deposit screen with VISA receipts for January 8 selected

Figure 7-2 Deposit Detail for January 8 VISA payments received

4. Change the date to reflect the date of the credit card payment receipts.

5. Enter in the ***VISA/MC Deposit*** in the memo field.

> **Tip:**
> Entering in a memo of "Amex deposit" or "VISA/MC deposit"
> will make it easier to differentiate the deposits from cash and
> check deposits when reconciling the bank statement.

6. Click **Save & Close** to record the deposit.

Repeat the steps for making deposits to record the American Express and any Discover or other credit card receipts.

If your credit card deposits are "net of discount fees," then you can record the discount fee as you make each deposit. This is typical of American Express. On the *Make Deposits* screen, enter a line at the bottom using the **Merchant Account Fees** account, as shown in Figure 7-3.

> **Tip:**
> Call your merchant processor and ask them to change to
> withdrawing merchant fees monthly. This saves time when
> recording deposit and makes accounting for the discount fees
> easier.

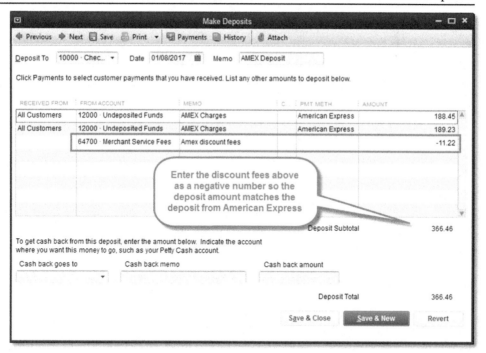

Figure 7-3 American Express Deposit with Discount Fees Deducted Daily

The accounting behind the scenes for credit card payments received is shown in Figure 7-4.

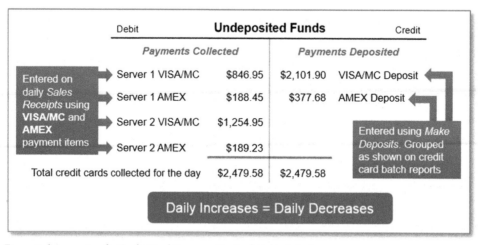

Figure 7-4 Accounting for Credit Card Payments Received, Behind the Scenes

Depositing Checks and Cash

The setup of your Cash/Check payment items determines the workflow for depositing cash and checks. If you have mapped the *Cash/Checks* payment items to the undeposited funds account, follow similar steps used for depositing credit cards.

1. Click **Banking > Make Deposits**.

2. Choose *Cash and Check* in the *View payment method type* drop-down list, as shown in Figure 7-5.

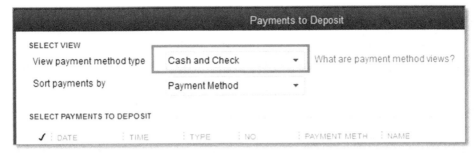

Figure 7-5 Payments to Deposit Window, Select Payment Method Type

3. Select all of the transactions for the day's deposit, and click **OK**.

4. Select the correct *Deposit to* account.

5. Enter the *Date* of the deposit.

6. Enter **cash/checks deposit** in the *memo* field. This memo will show up when reconciling to make it easier to differentiate this deposit from a credit card deposit.

7. Click **Save & Close** to record the deposit.

For restaurants that do not deposit cash on a daily basis, use a *Cash* payment item mapped to the *Cash on Hand* account, which is a cash fund on the premises usually kept in the safe; there is no extra step to record the funds being "deposited" into the safe.

The accounting behind the scenes for the *Cash on Hand* account when cash is not run through the *Undeposited Funds* account is shown in Figure 7-6.

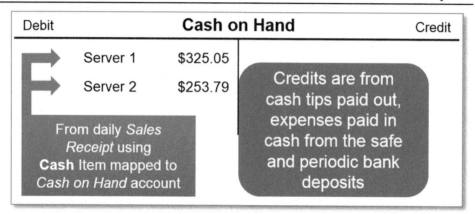

Figure 7-6 Accounting Behind the Scenes, Cash on Hand Account

Any checks that are received through the POS system will be recorded on the daily *Sales Receipt* using the *Checks* payment item, which is mapped to *Undeposited Funds*. Follow the steps listed above to group the checks so they match the amount deposited to the bank.

Depositing House Account Payments

Checks received from customers who have house accounts are automatically posted to *Undeposited Funds* based on the preferences set in the *Payments Preferences*, discussed on page 11. This allows for the house account payments to be grouped along with the check payments posted on the daily *Sales Receipts* (and cash payments if you are depositing cash daily).

The goal is to ensure that the payment amounts recorded in QuickBooks are grouped together so they match the exact amount recorded on the bank statement.

Chapter 8
Managing Expenses

QuickBooks provides several features to keep track of and manage company expenses, including entering and paying bills, writing checks, paying sales tax, using company credit cards, keeping track of 1099 reporting needs, and managing cash paid out of the register. These features allow you to track expenses in detail and create extensive reports that help manage vendor relationships and control costs in your business. We will provide an overview of these topics in this chapter.

The *Vendors* section of the *Home* page window provides a graphical flow of the steps involved in managing vendors, purchases, and payments. Clicking the **Vendors** icon on the *Home* page or the *Icon Bar* displays the *Vendor Center*. The *Vendor Center* displays information about all of your vendors and their transactions in a single place. From here you can add new vendors, add transactions to an existing vendor, and print list and transaction information.

Setting up Vendors

Vendors include every person or company from whom you purchase products or services, including trade vendors, service vendors, and 1099 contract workers. Before recording any transactions to a Vendor in QuickBooks, you must set them up in the *Vendor Center*.

> **Tip:**
> When a vendor is also a customer, you should set up two separate records: a vendor record in the *Vendor Center* and a customer record in the *Customer Center*. The customer name must be slightly different from the vendor name. For example, you could enter XYZ Company as "XYZ Company-V" for the vendor name in the *New Vendor* window, and "XYZ Company-C" for the customer name in the *New Customer* window. The contact information for both customer and vendor record can be identical.

To set up a new vendor, follow these steps:

1.   Open the Vendor Center.

2.   Click the **New Vendor** button and choose **New Vendor** from the drop-down menu as shown in Figure 8-1.

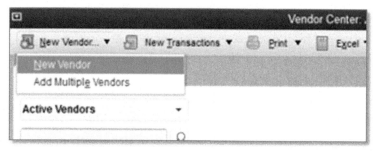

Figure 8-1 Add New Vendor

3.   Fill in as much information as desired on the following tabs: Address Info, Payment Settings, Tax Settings, Account Settings, and Additional Info.

> **Tip:**
> The *Vendor List* sorts alphabetically, just like the *Customer List*. Therefore, if your vendor is an individual person, enter the last name first, followed by the first name.
>
> **Note:**
> If you set up vendor types as described on page 39, add them to the *Additional Info* tab when setting up vendors.

1099 Tracking

The Internal Revenue Service requires any business that pays $600 or more for services in a calendar year to issue a form 1099-MISC to the recipient. This includes cash and check payments. Credit card payments are exempt from this requirement. Recipients that are incorporated are generally not eligible to receive a 1099-MISC form, with the exception of legal fees paid to corporations. For more information on the requirements for preparing forms 1099-MISC, visit IRS.gov.

In order to determine whether or not you are required to issue a 1099 form, you will need to obtain a signed IRS form W-9 from each of the vendors that provide a service to the restaurant. This includes but is not limited to live entertainment services, janitorial services, consulting services, and repairs and maintenance.

QuickBooks will help you keep track of the amounts to be included on the 1099-MISC forms. You can also use QuickBooks to prepare the forms that are sent to the recipients and the IRS.

In order to use the built-in 1099 form functionality, enter the correct information from the Form W-9 in the *Tax Settings* tab, as shown in Figure 8-2.

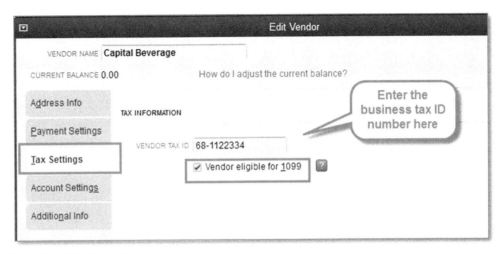

Figure 8-2 1099 Tax Settings

More information on processing 1099 forms can be found in our *QuickBooks Complete Textbook*, available at The Sleeter Group's online store.

Paying Vendors Using QuickBooks

With QuickBooks, you can pay your vendors in several ways. You can pay by check, credit card, electronic funds transfer, or, though not recommended, from your cash on hand (sometimes referred to as Petty Cash).

Most of the time, you'll pay your vendors from a checking account, so this section covers three different situations for recording payments out of your checking account. The three situations are:

- Manually writing a check or initiating an electronic funds transfer and recording the transaction in a QuickBooks account register.

- Using the *Write Checks* function to record and print checks.

- Recording accounts payable bills through the *Enter Bills* window and using the *Pay Bills* function to pay these *Bills*.

Using Registers

Aside from printing checks directly out of QuickBooks (discussed later in this chapter), there are several ways that money can come out of the company's bank account. Handwritten checks, electronic funds transfers (EFT), ATM charges, and Debit Card transactions are some examples. These withdrawals need to be entered into the QuickBooks file so you can reconcile the bank account. Bank reconciliations are discussed later in this book.

To enter handwritten checks, EFTs, ATM charges, and Debit Card transaction into the QuickBooks register, follow these steps:

1. Select the **Check Register** icon from the *Home* page or press **Ctrl+R** on your keyboard and select the appropriate **Bank Account**.

2. Enter the date the check was written or the date of the EFT/ATM/Debit Card withdrawal in the *Date* column.

3. Enter the actual check number in the *number* field or use *EFT, ATM, Debit*, or some other identifier in the number field.

4. In the *Payee* column, enter the name of the vendor to whom the expense was paid.

    If the vendor is not in the *Vendor List*, QuickBooks prompts you to *Quick Add* or *Set Up* the vendor. By clicking on **Set Up**, you will follow the steps for Setting up Vendors discussed earlier in the chapter.

5. Click **Quick Add**. QuickBooks will add this vendor without entering the address or other vendor information. You can always go back later and add the other information by editing the vendor record. In the *Select Name Type* dialog box, the *Vendor* name type is selected. Click **OK** to add the new vendor name to the *Vendor Center*.

6. Enter the amount of the payment in the *Payment* column.

7. Enter the desired expense account name in the *Account* column, such as **Office Supplies**.

8. Enter a memo to further designate what the expense was for, such as **Printer paper and toner**.

9. Verify that you've entered all of the fields in the transaction correctly, and click **Record** to save the transaction.

QuickBooks automatically updates the account balance in the register after you record the transaction.

Note:
To split your purchase to more than one account, move your cursor to the transaction in the register and click anywhere on the line to select the transaction. Click the **Splits** button in the lower left corner of the *Register* and add additional lines as needed.

Using Write Checks Without Using Accounts Payable

An alternative to entering manual checks and other withdrawals from the bank account through the *Register* is to use the *Write Checks* form. It is a personal preference as to which method you choose to use. By using the *Write Checks* form, it looks more like an actual check. Entering the split lines is easier with the *Write Checks* form.

If you want to keep track of vendor bill numbers and pay multiple bills with one check, you will want to use the accounts payable feature discussed later in this chapter.

To enter checks with the *Write Checks* form, follow these steps:

1. Display the *Write Checks* window by clicking on the **Write Checks** icon on the *Home* page, or by pressing **Ctrl+W** on your keyboard.

2. Select the correct bank account from the *Account* field.

3. Select the *Print Later* checkbox at the top of the window if you would like to print this check from QuickBooks.

    If you don't want to print this check and prefer to enter in the handwritten check number or **EFT/ATM/Debit** as the reference number, be sure *Print Later* is not selected, and enter the reference in the *No.* field.

4.   Enter the *Date*, *Vendor*, *Amount*, *Account*, and *Memo* in the appropriate fields.

5.   Click **Save & Close** when you have completed the check entry.

> **Note:**
> If you recorded the check with a **To Print** status, you can print it later, perhaps in a batch with other checks. If you want to print the check immediately after you enter it, you would click **Print** at the top of the *Write Checks* window and select *Check*. QuickBooks will ask you to enter the check number. To print a group of checks, use **File > Print Forms > Checks**.

Managing Accounts Payable

You can use QuickBooks to track Accounts Payable (A/P). When you receive a bill from a vendor, enter it into QuickBooks using the *Enter Bills* window. Recording a *Bill* allows QuickBooks to track the amount you owe to the vendor along with the details of what you purchased and the date the bill is due. For a *Bill* to be considered paid by QuickBooks, you must pay it using the *Pay Bills* window

Entering Bills

When a bill arrives from your vendor, enter it into QuickBooks using the *Enter Bills* icon on the *Home* page, as shown in Figure 8-3.

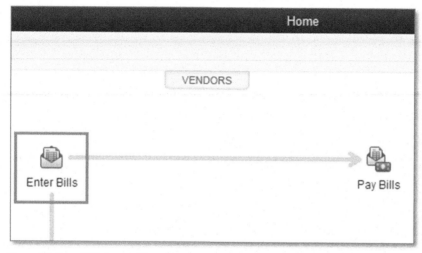

Figure 8-3 Enter Bills Icon on Home Page

Enter in the appropriate vendor and bill information on the *Bill* form, as shown in Figure 8-4.

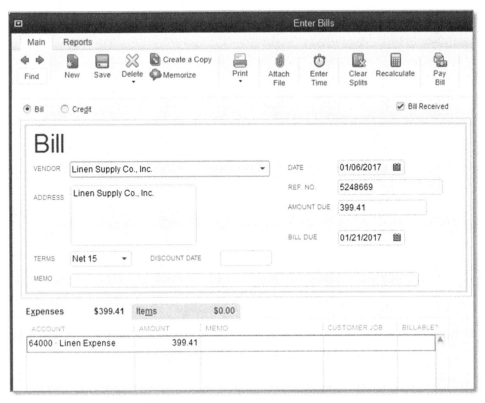

Figure 8-4 Enter Linen Supply Bill

Attaching Documents

There are many advantages to storing documents electronically. Going "paperless" increases efficiency and eliminates costly storage.

QuickBooks allows you to attach electronic documents to QuickBooks transactions, such as *Bills*, *Invoices*, and other QuickBooks forms. The attached documents can be stored on your system for free. To attach electronic documentation to a QuickBooks transaction, look for the *Attach* button in the upper section of the transaction window as show in Figure 8-5.

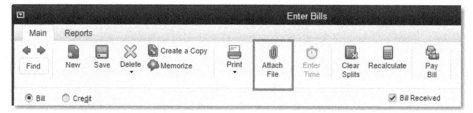

Figure 8-5 Attach Button in Enter Bills Window

Unpaid Bills Report

To see a list of all of the bills entered but not paid, click on **Reports >
Vendors & Payables > Unpaid Bills Detail**. This will display a list of all
bills and bill credits by vendor, as shown in Figure 8-6.

Type	Date	Num	Due Date	Aging	Open Balance
AT & T					
Bill	01/15/2017	12/20-1/15 stmt	01/25/2017		1,158.16
Total AT & T					1,158.16
Brand Management LLC					
Bill	01/10/2017	2548	01/25/2017		1,000.00
Total Brand Management LLC					1,000.00
California Choice					
Bill	01/02/2017	Jan Premium	01/10/2017	7	4,000.00
Total California Choice					4,000.00
Linen Supply Co., Inc.					
Bill	01/06/2017	5248669	01/21/2017		399.41
Bill	01/13/2017	5248874	01/28/2017		409.17
Total Linen Supply Co., Inc.					808.58
National Restaurant Association					
Bill	01/10/2017	Renewal	01/31/2017		620.00
Total National Restaurant Association					620.00
Restaurant Supply Inc.					
Credit	01/17/2017	3403			-350.00
Bill	01/13/2017	3392	01/23/2017		1,350.00
Total Restaurant Supply Inc.					1,000.00
Sacramento County					
Bill	01/02/2017	2017 Bus Lic	01/25/2017		200.00
Total Sacramento County					200.00
Sysco					
Bill	01/04/2017	101694	01/14/2017	3	6,202.85
Bill	01/11/2017	102010	01/21/2017		5,910.16
Total Sysco					12,113.01
TOTAL					20,899.75

AcademyRestaurant2015
Unpaid Bills Detail
As of January 17, 2017

Figure 8-6 Unpaid Bills Detail Report

Paying Bills

QuickBooks keeps track of all your bills in the Accounts Payable account. When you pay your bills, you will reduce the balance in Accounts Payable by creating *Bill Payment* checks.

By using the *Enter Bills* and *Pay Bills* features, you will be able to provide the vendor with a list of the invoices that were paid on a particular check.

To pay vendor bills, follow these steps:

1. Select the **Pay Bills** icon on the *Home* page as shown in Figure 8-7 to display a list of all unpaid bills.

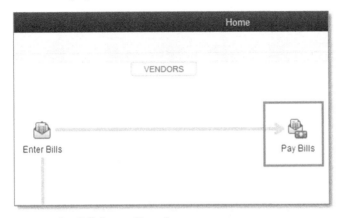

Figure 8-7 Pay Bills Icon on Home Page

2. Select the bills you want to pay by placing a check mark in the left hand column, as shown in Figure 8-8.

3. Choose **Check** as the payment method.

4. Select the correct bank account.

5. When all of the bills to be paid are selected, click on **Pay Selected Bills** to record the *Bill Payments.*

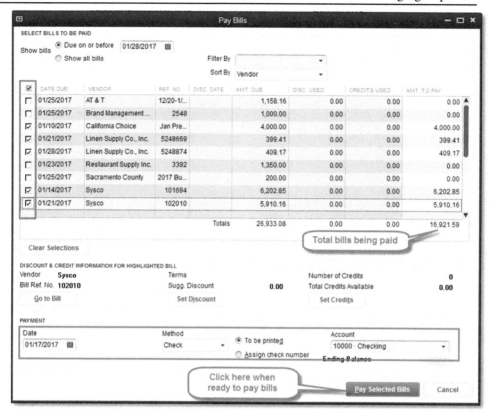

Figure 8-8 Pay Bills window

6.   QuickBooks displays a *Payment Summary* dialog box as shown in Figure
      8-9. From here you can print checks on preprinted check stock as described
      below.

Figure 8-9 Bill Payment Summary dialog box

Printing Checks

By clicking on **Print Checks** as shown in Figure 8-9, QuickBooks displays the *Select Checks to Print* window as shown in Figure 8-10. Confirm the checks to print, enter the *First Check Number*, and click **OK**.

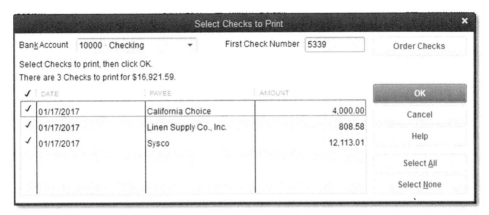

Figure 8-10 Select Checks to Print

> **Note:**
> If you select more than one *Bill* for the same vendor, QuickBooks combines all of the amounts onto a single *Bill Payment*.

The *Print Checks* window shown in Figure 8-11 is displayed. Select your printer from the drop-down menu. Ensure the proper *Check Style* is selected. By using the *voucher style checks*, you will have two check stubs. One can be left attached to the check and sent to the vendor with the bill payment information listed. The other stub becomes the restaurant's copy.

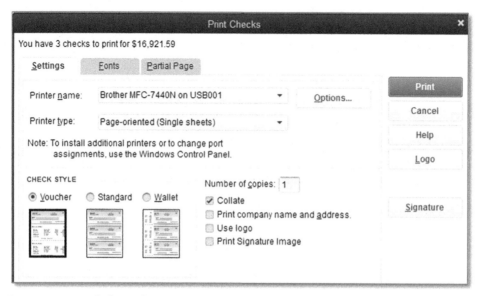

Figure 8-11 Print Checks Window

> **Tips:**
> 1. Make sure your checks are oriented correctly in the printer. With some printers, you feed the top of the page in first, while with others you feed in bottom first. With some printers, you must insert the check face up, and with others, face down.
>
> 2. If you are paying several bills on a single check and the bill details won't fit on one check stub, you can print a *Bill Payment Stub* by choosing **Bill Payment Stub** from the *Print Forms* submenu on the *File* menu.

After the checks are printed, ensure that the check numbers on the *Print Checks – Confirmation* window match the actual check numbers printed. If they all match up, click **OK**. Ensuring that the check numbers are accurate makes the bank reconciliation process much smoother. If the numbers don't match up, select the checks to be reprinted and then go into the *Register* for the bank account and enter the correct check numbers.

Voiding Checks

QuickBooks allows you to keep the information about voided checks so that you retain a record of these checks. It is important to enter each check into your register even if the check is voided. This will prevent gaps in your check number sequence.

> **Note:**
> If your printer damages your checks during the printing process, it is best accounting practice to void each damaged check and re-enter a new check in the bank account register, the *Write Checks* window, or by using the *Pay Bills* feature.

To void checks, follow these steps:

1. Open the **Checking** account register and then select the check by clicking anywhere on that record. You will be able to tell that the record has been selected, as it will be outlined in the register.

2. From the *Edit* menu, select **Void Bill Payment Check** or **Void Check**, depending on the type of transaction you are voiding. When you void a check, QuickBooks changes the amount to zero, marks the check cleared, and adds *VOID* to the *Memo* field.

3. Click **Record** to save your changes.

4. If you are voiding a *Bill Payment* check, QuickBooks warns you that this change will affect the application of this check to the *Bills*, as shown in Figure 8-12. In other words, voiding a *Bill Payment* will make the *Bills* payable again. To issue a new check for these bills, use the *Pay Bills* feature and re-select the bills for payment.

5. Click **Yes** to accept the warning.

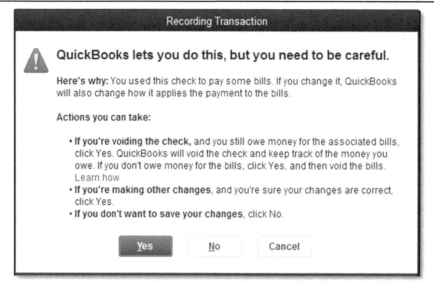

Figure 8-12 Recording Transaction dialog box about voiding BILLPMT check

If you are voiding a check number that has never been entered, use the *Write Checks* feature. Use the steps described above to void the check, ensuring that the correct check number is displayed. Enter an *account* name in the *expenses* tab before saving the voided check.

> **Did You Know?**
> QuickBooks has a special report called *Missing Checks* that allows you to view all of your checks sorted by check number. The report highlights any duplicate check numbers and gaps in the check number sequence. To view this report, select the **Reports** menu, then select **Banking**, and then select **Missing Checks**.

Applying Vendor Credits

When a vendor credits your account, you should record the transaction in the *Enter Bills* window as a *Credit* and apply it to one or more of your unpaid *Bills*.

To create a vendor credit, follow these steps:

1.   Click on the **Enter Bills** icon on the *Home* page.

2.   Select the *Credit* radio button at the top of left of the window as shown in Figure 8-13.

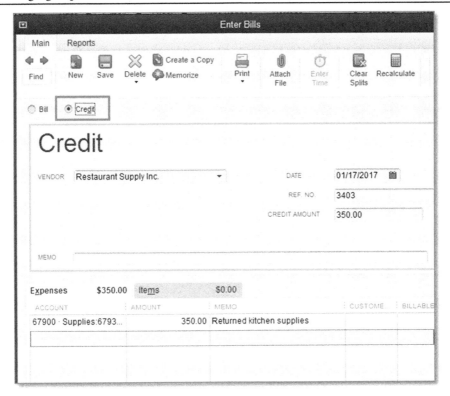

Figure 8-13 Enter Vendor Credit

3.   Fill in the *Bill Credit* information using the correct vendor name, date, reference number amount, and account.

You can easily see which vendors have open credits by running the *Unpaid Bills Detail* report as discussed on page 96.

To apply the *Bill Credit* to a *Bill* for a vendor, follow these steps:

1.   Select **Pay Bills** from the *Home* page.

2.   Select the vendor bill you want to apply the credit to by selecting it with a check mark on the left hand side, as shown in Figure 8-14.

Note:
When you select a *Bill* from a vendor for whom one or more unapplied credits exist, QuickBooks displays the total amount of all credits for the vendor in the *Total Credits Available* section. Notice the credit of $350.00 shown in Figure 8-14.

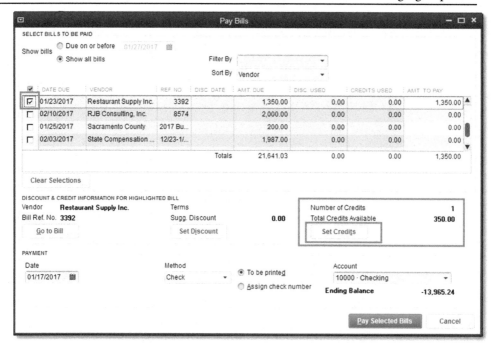

Figure 8-14 Set Vendor Bill Credits

3.   Click **Set Credits**. In the *Discounts and Credits* window, QuickBooks automatically selected the credits to be applied to the *Bill*. You can override what is shown by deselecting the credit (removing the checkmark), or by entering a different amount in the *Amt. To Use* column.

4.   Leave the credit selected as shown in Figure 8-15 and click **Done**.

     QuickBooks has applied the $350.00 credit to Bill #3392 and reduced the amount in the *Amt. To Pay* column to $1,000.00

5.   Click **Pay Selected Bills** to pay the bill.

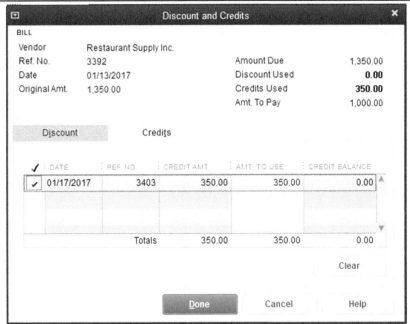

Figure 8-15 Discounts and Credits window to set Bill Credit

6.   Click **Done** on the *Payment Summary dialog box* and follow the prompts to print the check.

> **Note:**
> If you want to apply the credit without paying the *Bill*, reduce the *Amt. To Pay* column to zero.

Tracking Cash Paid Out of Register

It is not uncommon for some restaurant suppliers to expect to be paid at the time of delivery. Whenever possible, checks should be written for restaurant expenditures. It is sometimes necessary to use cash for restaurant expenditures, such as a quick run to the grocery store to pick up food items the restaurant may have run out of, payments to vendors who will not accept checks, or suppliers who do not grant the restaurant credit terms.

In order to track these expenditures, you will use a clearing account in QuickBooks called *Paid Outs Clearing*. As discussed on page 16, the *Paid Outs Clearing* account is a *Bank* account. Using a *Bank* type of account allows for expenses to be entered in the *Register* or with the *Write Checks* form so you can capture vendor information and track the expenditures more easily.

The POS system should have a way to capture the amounts paid out in cash from the day's sales. Recording the amounts paid out in cash on the daily *Sales Receipt* is discussed on page 66.

As part of the daily accounting procedures in QuickBooks, you will need to post the details of the expenses that were paid out of the register. To capture this information, the restaurant staff submits actual receipts for each and every paid out. It is important that the receipts be maintained by the business to substantiate the expenses.

The goal of the *Paid Outs Clearing* account is to have it always maintain a zero balance. The accounting behind the scenes is shown in Figure 8-16.

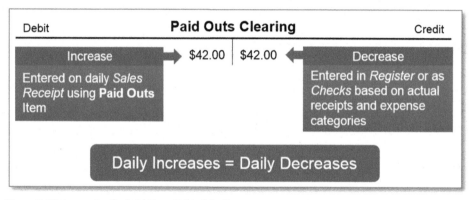

Figure 8-16 Accounting for Paid Outs, Behind the Scenes

In order to record the cash paid outs, follow the Using Registers steps listed on page 92, or the Using Write Checks Without Using Accounts Payable steps listed on page 93.

Tip:
In the event that a *Bill* entered in QuickBooks was paid by cash from the register, you can use the same steps described for paying bills on page 97 and choose the *Paid Outs Clearing* account as the *Bank* account. This will mark the bill as paid and clear out the *Paid Outs Clearing* account.

Figure 8-17 shows the details for the *Paid Outs Clearing* account after all of the receipts for cash paid outs have been recorded.

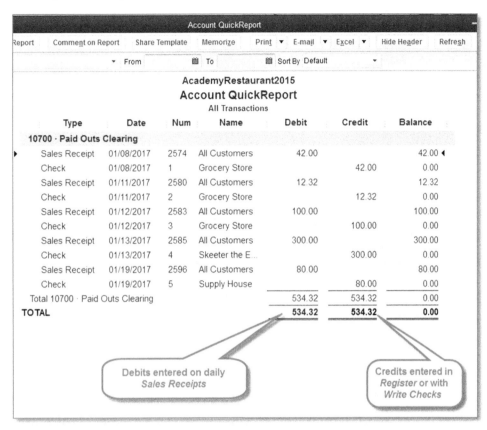

Figure 8-17 Paid Outs Clearing Account Transaction Details

> **Note:**
> The *Paid Outs Clearing* account is different from the *Cash on Hand* account. *Paid Outs Clearing* always has a zero balance while the restaurant may actually have cash on the premises that was not deposited to the bank.

Paying Vendors Using Bill.com

What Is Bill.com?

Bill.com is an online application that handles the processing of accounts payable and accounts receivable transactions. In this section, we will discuss the accounts payable features of Bill.com. For more information on Bill.com, including accounts receivable and cash forecasting, refer to *Grow Your Accounting Practice Using Bill.com*, by Judie McCarthy, which is published by The Sleeter Group and is available in our online store.

Overview

The accounts payable process using QuickBooks alone requires several manual steps:

- Mailed paper bills are opened and date stamped as received.

- Emailed bills need to be printed and date-stamped as received.

- Bills are routed to a manager for approval and then sent to the bookkeeper.

- Once approved, the bookkeeper enters the *Bill* into QuickBooks and files the paper bill in a *pending* file folder waiting for payment to be made.

- When it is time to pay bills, a report is generated so the manager can decide which bills need to be paid.

- Once the bills to pay are determined, the bookkeeper creates the checks in QuickBooks.

- The checks are printed and bills are pulled from the pending file and routed to an authorized signer for signature.

- After the checks are signed, they are routed back to the bookkeeper so the checks can put in envelopes, stamped, and mailed.

- The bill payment stubs are then attached to the paper bills that were paid.

- Finally, the paid bills are filed away in the filing cabinet.

Your process may be a little different, but it still involves multiple steps and a lot of paper pushing.

Bill.com simplifies this whole accounts payable process by eliminating the need to push paper around. The process becomes much more streamlined and involves fewer steps:

- Bills are faxed, emailed, or uploaded to the restaurant's Bill.com inbox.

- Bill details are entered, the bill is filed electronically in Bill.com, and one or more approvers can be notified that bills need to be approved.

- Approvers can review the electronic copies and accept or reject the bill, including notes about why they are not approving the bill for payment.

- Upon approval, bill payments can be scheduled today for automatic payment in the future by paper check or e-payment.

- The bills and bill payments are sync'd to QuickBooks.

By using Bill.com, there is no need to route paper around the office or print and mail checks. All documents related to the bill payment are easily found in Bill.com and all documents are searchable. As shown in Figure 8-18, the accounts payable process is streamlined by using Bill.com.

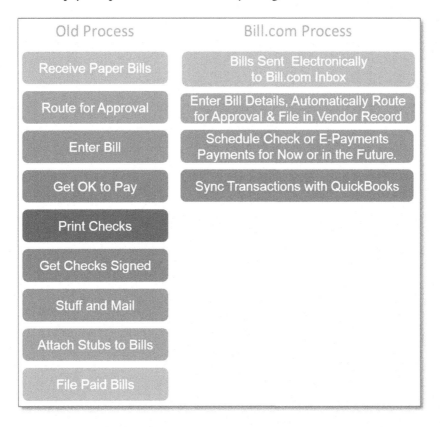

Figure 8-18 Old Bill Payment Process vs. Bill.com Process

Benefits

Bill.com provides a number of benefits to the restaurant. These benefits include:

- *Time Savings* - Rather than touching the paper bills several times during the process, Bill.com saves time by not requiring so many steps in the bill pay process. This frees up the bookkeeper and managers to do other things.

- *Document Storage* - Any electronic documents can be stored in the Bill.com portal, including bank statements, PDF files, Word files, Excel files, or any other electronic documents. At this time there are no limits on the number or size of data files that can be stored with Bill.com.

- *Documents are Easily Retrievable* - Not only does the electronic storage of documents free up storage space in the filing cabinets, the documents can be retrieved easily in the case of an audit. Bill.com can put all of your documents, including bills and cancelled checks, on an indexed CD for a nominal fee.

- *Anywhere Access* - Bills can be approved for payment from anywhere there is an Internet connection by using a connected laptop, iPad (or other tablet), or even from a mobile phone using the Bill.com app. It is not necessary for the bookkeeper or approvers to be in the same building to manage accounts payable.

- *Audit Trail* - A full audit trail shows who entered the bills, who approved the bills, and who paid the bills.

- *Data Sync* - Data sync with QuickBooks means no double entry.

- *Payment Batching* - When a dozen vendors are paid on the same day, Bill.com batches the payments together and pulls one amount from your bank account. The checks are then issued on a trust account, so vendors and other third parties will not have access to the restaurant's bank account information. This reduces the risk of having the bank account compromised.

- *Easier Bank Reconciliation* - The batching of payments for the day means the bank account reconciliation is much easier because you have one amount to reconcile instead of 12 individual checks.

- *Uncleared Check Monitoring* - If checks go uncleared for 20 days, Bill.com will notify you so you can contact the vendor. Voiding and reissuing the check is quick and easy.

- *User Roles* - User roles can be customized so the same person entering the bills is not the person who pays the bills.

- *Approvals* - Approval policies can be customized to ensure that no bills are changed after they have been approved.

Tracking Company Credit Cards

QuickBooks allows you to track charges and payments on your company credit card, reconcile the balance on your statement to the balance in QuickBooks and pay the bill in full, or make partial payments on the balance due. Using the credit card feature allows you to record the transactions as they occur and post the payment to the credit card liability account, whether you make a partial payment or pay the entire balance in full each month.

Setting Up Credit Card Account

Create a new *Credit Card* type of account in the *Chart of Accounts* list for each card by clicking **Lists > Chart of Accounts** and clicking **Ctrl+N** to add a new account. The account should resemble Figure 8-19.

If you have multiple credit card accounts, we recommend adding the last four digits of the card to the end of the *Account Name* to differentiate the charges. Credit card slips generally include the last four digits, and having this number in the account name makes posting the charges easier.

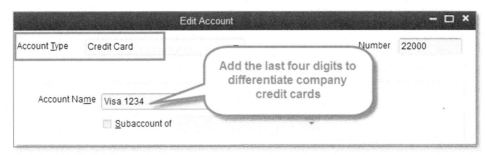

Figure 8-19 Add Credit Card Account

Entering Credit Card Charges

Enter each charge individually by clicking on **Banking > Enter Credit Card Charges**. The form is very similar to a *Bill* or *Write Checks* form. Fill in the appropriate fields. Choose the *Credit Card* account used and whether it was a purchase or return. Enter the vendor name in the *Purchased From* field along with the appropriate information in the date, reference, amount, memo, and expense account fields. Click **Save & Close** when finished, or **Save & New** to add more credit card charges. The charges will look similar to Figure 8-20.

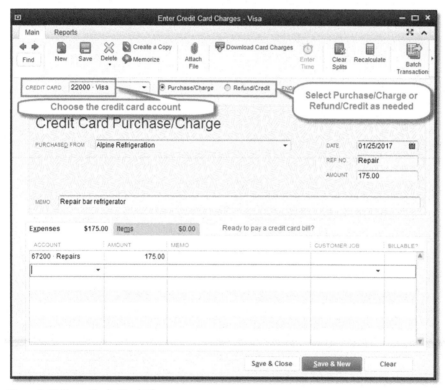

Figure 8-20 Enter Credit Card Charges

Recording Vendor Bills Paid by Credit Card

If a *Bill* was entered in QuickBooks and paid by the company credit card instead of a company check, follow the steps for paying bills as described on page 97 with the following changes:

Instead of choosing the *Check* payment method, change this to *Credit Card* as shown in Figure 8-21 and choose the correct *Credit Card* in the *Account* field.

Figure 8-21 Pay Bills by Credit Card

Reconciling the Credit Card Statement

Reconciling the credit card statement involves the same steps as reconciling the bank account. This is covered in detail starting on page 129. After reading Chapter 10 – Reconciling the Bank Account, you will understand how to reconcile the credit card account. The only difference is that you will enter in the interest charged by the credit card company on the *Begin Reconciliation* screen, as shown in Figure 8-22.

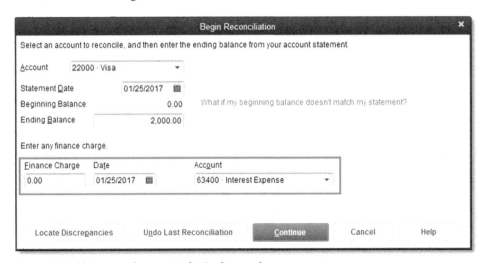

Figure 8-22 Add Finance Charge to Credit Card Reconciliation

Paying the Credit Card Bill

By entering in the charges using the credit card feature, QuickBooks is debiting the expense account and crediting the *VISA* account. When you pay the bill, you will be using *VISA* as the expense account no matter how you record the payment

To record the payment of the credit card bill, you have the following options:

1. If the payment is made online through the credit card company website, you can enter the transaction in the register as described on page 92 or use the write check method describe on page 93. For both methods, enter the date of the payment, vendor, amount, and the appropriate credit card account as the expense account.

2. You can enter a *Bill* for the amount that will be paid. Enter the statement date as the bill *Date*, enter the payment due date from the statement as the due date on the bill, and enter *VISA* as the expense account.

    Avoid the temptation to enter a bill for the full balance of the statement and partial pay the bill. This will cause problems when reconciling because the bill amount is what shows up as a payment in the *Reconcile* window. To ensure a smooth reconciliation process, enter the bill for the amount of the partial payment. Your *Bill* should resemble Figure 8-23.

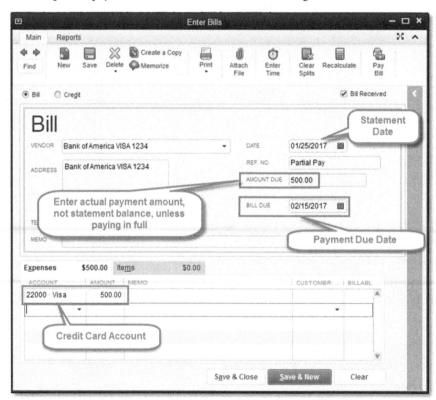

Figure 8-23 Enter Bill for Credit Card Payment

> **Note:**
> Setting up a separate vendor for each credit card with the last
> four digits of the card will help segregate payment activity for
> each card.

Managing Sales Tax

State tax laws vary in their treatment of food and beverages for sales tax
purposes. Your POS system should be set up to ensure you are taxing your
menu items correctly so you can collect and remit the right amount of sales
tax. In many states, aside from the state tax, each county or city may impose
an additional tax that businesses are required to track and report.

If you sell non-taxable food and beverage items, your state will probably
require both a breakdown of non-taxable sales and also the reason sales tax
was not imposed.

These differing conditions may not apply in all jurisdictions, but QuickBooks
allows you to track sales tax for all of these different situations. If you are not
familiar with the sales tax rates or reporting requirements in your area, consult
your state agency, your local QuickBooks ProAdvisor, or your accountant for
guidance.

For your sales tax return, we recommend that you use the total sales and
taxable sales from your POS system. However, to track your sales tax liability
on the Balance Sheet, set up *Sales Tax Items* as discussed on page 34. If set up
properly, QuickBooks will provide you with the information needed to file
your sales tax returns.

Sales Tax Items

In Chapter 2 – Setting up QuickBooks for Restaurants, we discussed how to
turn on the sales tax feature and how to set up the items for tracking sales tax.
If you have restaurants in multiple locations, set up additional *Sales Tax Items*
for each jurisdiction.

> **Note:**
> If you remit sales tax to **only one agency** (e.g., California's State Board of Equalization) but you collect sales tax in several different counties or cities, create a separate *Sales Tax Item* for each taxable location in which you sell products. This allows you to track different sales tax rates for each locale.
>
> **Note:**
> If you pay sales tax to **more than one agency**, you should use *Sales Tax Group*s to combine several different *Sales Tax Items* into a group tax rate.

Sales Tax Revenue Summary

The sales information that was entered with the daily *Sales Receipts* is used to calculate the amounts to report on the sales tax return. Items like *Gift Certificate Sales, Tips Collected, House Account Charges,* and *Cash Over/Short* will be listed as *Excluded*. The *Taxable Sales* and *Non-Taxable Sales* columns are likely what will be used on your sales tax return.

It is critical that you enter the correct subtotal on the daily *Sales Receipts* as described in Chapter 5 – Recording Daily Sales , or your sales tax reports will not calculate correctly.

To create the *Sales Tax Revenue Summary* report, click **Reports > Vendors & Payables > Sales Tax Revenue Summary**. Change the dates to the desired time period. The example in Figure 8-24 shows this report for a two-week period in January 2017.

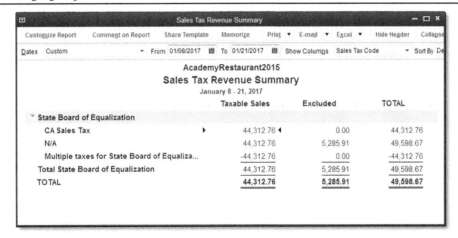

Figure 8-24 Sales Tax Revenue Summary

It is a good idea to compare your total sales on the *Profit & Loss* report with the sales reported on the *Sales Tax Revenue Summary*, as shown in Figure 8-25, to ensure that the total sales are reported correctly.

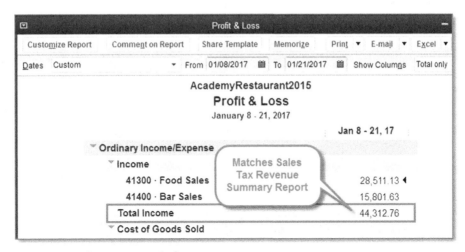

Figure 8-25 Total Income per Profit & Loss Report

If you have any questions about sales tax reporting, contact the appropriate state's revenue agency or your tax advisor.

Sales Tax Liability Report

To find out the total sales tax due, click **Reports > Vendors & Payables > Sales Tax Liability**. The dates default to *Last Month*. To run the report for a quarter or for the year, change the dates accordingly. The example in Figure 8-26 shows a two-week period in January 2017.

The *Tax Collected* column will provide the amount of sales tax collected for each sales tax jurisdiction during the period, as shown in Figure 8-26. This should match the amount due when you prepare your sales tax return.

> **Note:**
> If all of your sales are taxable, you may be able to use only the *Sales Tax Liability* report to prepare your sales tax return. If you have taxable and non-taxable sales, you will need the *Sales Tax Revenue Summary* report to differentiate non-taxable sales from excluded sales, which are not reportable.

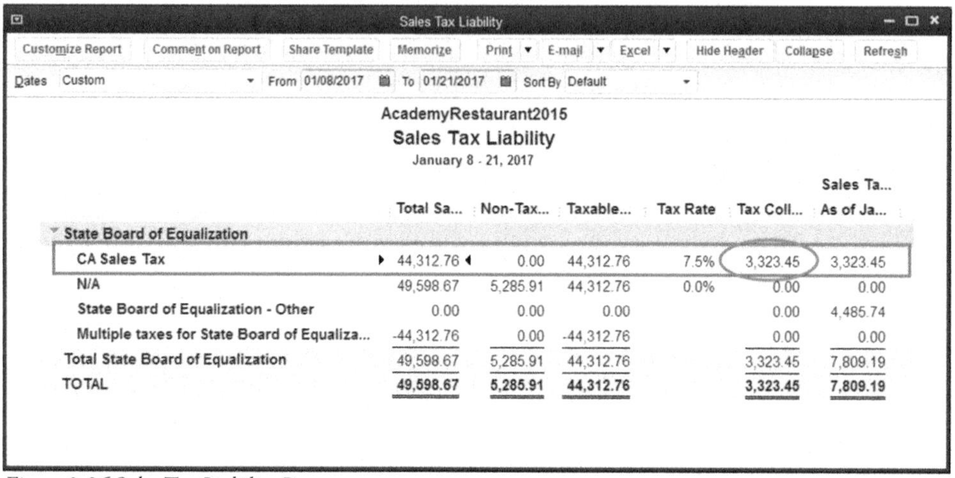

Figure 8-26 Sales Tax Liability Report

Adjusting Sales Tax

If you encounter a small rounding difference, you can adjust the total sales tax due before creating the payment by clicking on **Vendors > Sales Tax > Adjust Sales Tax Due**, as shown in Figure 8-27. Adjusting the sales tax liability ensures that the correct balance is shown on the Balance Sheet.

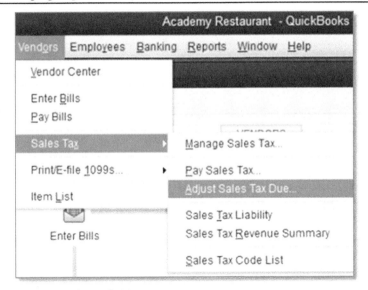

Figure 8-27 Adjust Sales Tax Due

Enter in the following information on the *Sales Tax Adjustment* screen:

- *Adjustment Date* is the end of the period you are adjusting.

- *Entry No.* will automatically populate.

- *Sales Tax Vendor* is the name of the agency to which the tax is paid.

- *Adjustment Account* can be whatever account type you choose. These adjustments should not be a material amount. In the restaurant sample file, we have created an *Other Expense* account called *Sales Tax Adjustments*.

- Decide whether to *Increase* or *Decrease Sales Tax By* and enter the amount of the adjustment.

Your completed adjustment should resemble Figure 8-28.

Figure 8-28 Sales Tax Adjustment

Paying Sales Tax

When you pay your sales tax, do not use the *Write Checks* window. In order for QuickBooks to properly track sales tax, use the *Pay Sales Tax* feature. This will ensure that the total liability is correct on the *Sales Tax Liability* reports.

To pay your sales tax liability using the *Pay Sales Tax* feature, follow these steps:

1. From the *Home* page, select the **Manage Sales Tax** icon.

2. Click the **Pay Sales Tax** button in the *Manage Sales Tax* dialog box. Alternatively, from the *Vendors* menu, select **Sales Tax** and then select **Pay Sales Tax**. The *Pay Sales Tax* window displays.

3. In the *Pay From Account* field, confirm that **Checking** is displayed and press **Tab**. You can change the account from which you wish to pay your sales tax by selecting the correct account from the drop-down list.

4. Enter the date of the payment in the *Check Date* field.

5.   Enter the correct date in the *Show sales tax due through* field. This is the last day of the sales tax reporting period. For example, if you are filing your sales tax return for the first month, enter the last day of January in this field.

> **Note:**
> QuickBooks shows the total tax you owe for each tax jurisdiction as well as any adjustments. To pay all the tax and the adjustments for all rows, click the **Pay All Tax** button. You can create a Sales Tax Adjustment by clicking Adjust on this screen to round the amount due.

6.   If you will be writing a check, enter the *Starting Check No.* in the appropriate box, or mark the *to be printed* box to print the check later, as shown in Figure 8-29.

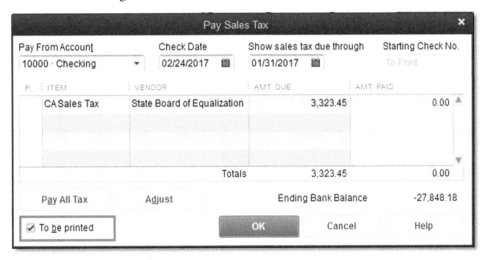

Figure 8-29 Pay Sales Tax Window

> **Note:**
> If you are paying your taxes online, do not enter a check number with this payment; instead, do the following:
>
> 1. Click the check box next to *To be Printed* and click **OK** to save the transaction.
>
> 2. Open the register as described in the Using Registers section of the Managing Expenses chapter.

3. Edit the check to reflect **ONLINE** or **EFT** as the check number and record the change.

Many states require you to file your sales tax online. We recommend preparing or e-filing your tax returns and recording the *Sales Tax Payment* in QuickBooks before the final submission. This ensures that the amount paid with the tax return matches the amount paid in QuickBooks, and that you don't have any large, unexplainable errors.

Chapter 9
Inventory and Costing Considerations

Managing and controlling food and beverage costs is critical to the success of your restaurant business. These controls are often thought of as inventory control, but they are actually food costing issues. While the inventory features of QuickBooks are well suited for tracking discrete items that are purchased and sold, they are not very well suited for handling the imprecise measurements and waste that is inherent in preparing food recipes in restaurants and determining food costs. If you buy a bag of red onions and some goes on a burger, some goes on a chicken sandwich, some goes in a soup, and some goes on a salad, managing this with inventory items would be problematic. If you try to use QuickBooks to track your restaurant inventory, you will spend a lot of time correcting for these imprecisions to keep your records accurate, and they will still be imprecise. For these reasons, we do not recommend using inventory items in QuickBooks.

Food Costing

It is important to do a cost analysis of your menu items to ensure that you are pricing food and beverages correctly. These calculations need to be done outside of the accounting system.

One basic method for calculating menu prices, but not the only method, involves knowing two things:

1. The cost of every single ingredient that is needed to make the entrée and any side dishes. This includes the lemon juice squeezed on the fish and spices used to prepare the dish. This cost excludes labor.
2. The desired food cost as a percent of sales. Ideally, you want the food cost to be 25-30% of the menu price of the item.

Once you know these two numbers, divide the food cost by the desired food cost percentage to arrive at a desired menu price as shown in Figure 9-1. This desired price needs to be reviewed to ensure that it is a competitive price and doesn't gouge the customers.

Figure 9-1 Menu Pricing Formula

A similar formula is used for pricing bar items, however the desired cost percentage is likely lower than the food cost percentage. Once you have determined your bar item costs, including garnishment and mixers, you can use the formula in Figure 9-1 to determine the appropriate selling price.

Adjusting the Financial Records

Although you won't be using QuickBooks to track inventory on a perpetual basis (i.e., as each purchase and sale happens), you will need to account for inventory values on your Balance Sheet and cost of goods sold on your Income Statement. As you are entering bills for food and beverage purchases, they are being recorded as expenses to the purchases account(s), but do not reflect the total cost of what was sold because some of the items purchased may be held as inventory.

Here is a simple way to update your inventory and cost of goods sold, and keep your financial statements up to date. Start by taking periodic physical inventory. We suggest taking inventory every four weeks, but you could do it every week, every quarter, or every year. The more often you adjust QuickBooks to reflect your true cost of goods, the better handle you will have on the profitability of the restaurant, and the better control you'll have over theft or excessive waste. Do the physical inventory on the same day of the week whenever possible so your reporting is consistent.

To prepare the journal entry to adjust inventory, you need to calculate the net change in the value of your inventory for each category of purchases you track, using the formula shown in Figure 9-2.

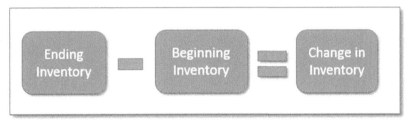

Figure 9-2 Change in Inventory Formula

To illustrate how to adjust inventory, let's look at some real numbers and apply the *Change in Inventory* formula.

Purchase Category	Inventory at End of Week	Inventory at Beginning of Week	Change in Inventory
Food	$5,563.17	$4,250.00	$1,313.17 Increase
Bar	$5,428.91	$5,428.91	$0.00
Totals	$10,992.08	$9,678.91	$1,313.17 Increase

Once you have determined the *Change in Inventory* for each purchase category as shown above, create a journal entry by clicking on **Company > Make General Journal Entries** to manually adjust the inventory, purchases, and adjusted cost of goods sold accounts. We recommend preparing one journal entry for each category of purchases. For illustration purposes, Bar inventory remained the same in the table above.

The first line of the journal entry affects the inventory account. If the *Net Change in Inventory* is positive, you need to debit inventory, and conversely if it's negative, you need to credit inventory.

> **Note:**
> Separate inventory accounts can be created for food and bar purchases if desired.

The second line of the journal entry affects the purchases account. Remove the balance in that account as of the date of the inventory count by crediting the appropriate purchases account (food or bar purchases), as shown in Figure 9-3.

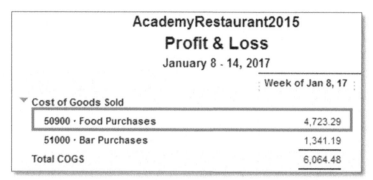

Figure 9-3 Inventory Adjustment, Food Purchases

> **Note:**
> Food and Bar purchases can be separate accounts or they can be combined into one account. Though it may be easier to use one account when entering supplier bills for purchases, separating them out will give you more insight into your financial reports.

The third line of the journal entry affects the adjusted cost of goods sold (COGS) account. The net difference between line one and line two is the balancing entry, which represents the actual cost of goods sold for the period. Enter in the debit or credit amount to *Food - Adjusted COGS* or *Bar Adjusted COGS* as appropriate.

> **Note:**
> If you have multiple purchases accounts, you need multiple *Adjusted COGS* accounts.

The entry shown in Figure 9-4 illustrates the food inventory adjustment for the week ending January 14, 2017.

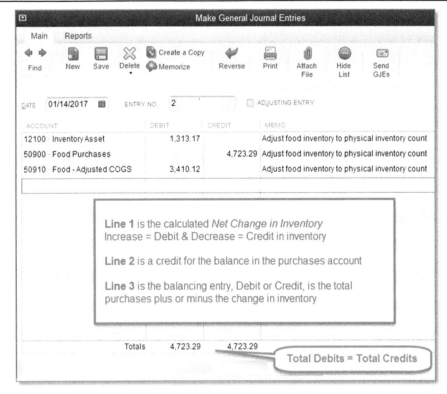

Figure 9-4 Adjusting Inventory for Periodic Physical Counts

After posting the inventory adjustment, the *Profit & Loss* Report should reflect a zero balance in the purchases account(s). The *Adjusted COGS* account(s) will reflect the total purchases +/- the net inventory change as shown in Figure 9-5.

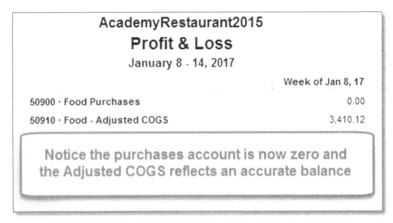

Figure 9-5 Purchases and Adjusted COGS after inventory entry

Repeat the process to adjust costs of goods sold and inventory for each purchase category that you are tracking.

Although QuickBooks is not the right tool for your detailed inventory and costing management, we still recommend using QuickBooks for all of your other accounting needs. You should use an inventory control software product to separately track detailed food and beverage costs and inventory.

Chapter 10
Reconciling the Bank Account

At the end of each month, you must reconcile the bank statement to the transactions entered into QuickBooks to ensure that everything in QuickBooks hits the bank and that everything that hits the bank is in QuickBooks. This is a very important step in the overall accounting process and ensures the accuracy of your accounting records.

In addition to reconciling bank accounts, you can also reconcile other accounts, such as credit card accounts, using the same process. In fact, you can reconcile almost any Other Current Asset, Fixed Asset, Credit Card, Other Current Liability, Long Term Liability, or Equity account using the same process presented in this chapter. However, even though QuickBooks *allows* you to reconcile many accounts, the primary accounts you'll reconcile are bank and credit card accounts, since these types of accounts always have monthly statements.

Matching Transactions in QuickBooks to the Bank Statement

Reconciling bank statements and credit card statements is basically identical, with a few changes in terminology shown on the *Reconcile* window. Before reconciling the account in QuickBooks, make sure you've entered all of the transactions for that account. For example, if you have automatic payments from your checking account (EFTs) or automatic charges on your credit card, it is best to enter those transactions before you start the reconciliation.

To reconcile the bank or credit card account, follow these steps:

1. From the *Home* page, click on the **Reconcile** Icon on the *Banking* section on the right hand side.

> **Note:**
> If the *Home* page is not already open, select the **Company** menu and then select **Home Page.**

2.   The *Begin Reconciliation* window opens as shown in Figure 10-1.

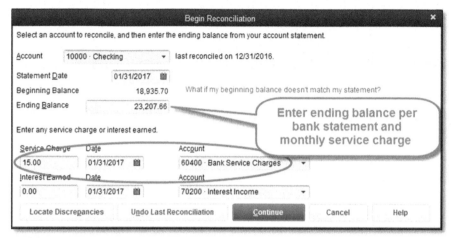

Figure 10-1 Begin Reconciliation

3.   The *Account* field already shows *Checking*. The account drop-down list allows you to select other accounts to reconcile. Press **Tab.**

4.   The *Statement Date* is the date listed on the bank or credit card statement. The default statement date is one month after your last reconciliation date.

5.   Look for the previous balance on the bank or credit card statement. Compare this amount with the *Beginning Balance* amount in the *Begin Reconciliation* window. Notice that they are the same.

> **Note:**
> QuickBooks calculates the *Beginning Balance* field in the *Begin Reconciliation* window by adding and subtracting all previously reconciled transactions. If the beginning balance does not match the bank statement, you probably made changes to previously cleared transactions. See *Finding Common Bank Reconciliation Errors* on page 134 for more information.

6.   Enter the ending balance from the bank or credit card statement in the *Ending Balance* field on the *Begin Reconciliation* window.

7. If there is a monthly service charge or interest reported on the bank
    statement or a finance charge reported on the credit card statement, and
    they have not been entered in QuickBooks, enter them on the *Begin
    Reconciliation* screen with the correct *Date* and *Account* and click
    Continue.

8. The *Reconcile – Checking* window will open as shown in Figure 10-2.

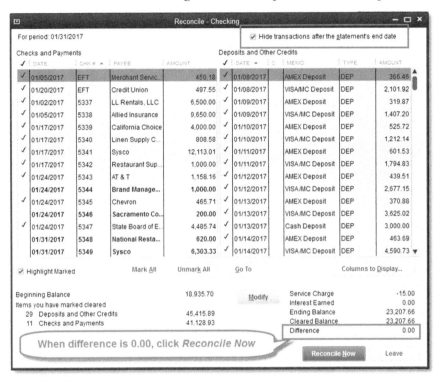

Figure 10-2 Reconcile, Checking Window

9. At the top of the *Reconcile* window, check the box labeled *Hide Transactions
    after the statement's end date*. This removes transactions dated after the
    statement date from being displayed on the screen. Since they could not
    possibly have cleared yet, this simplifies your life since you only have to
    look at transactions that *could* have cleared as of the statement date.

10. In the *Deposits and Other Credits* section on the right side of the *Reconcile*
    window, match the deposits and other credits on the bank statement with
    the associated QuickBooks transactions. In the case of a credit card
    reconciliation, the right side shows *Payments and Credits*. Click anywhere

on a line to mark it cleared. The checkmark (✔) indicates which
transactions have cleared.

11.   In the *Checks and Payments* section on the left side of the *Reconcile* window,
       match the checks and other withdrawals on the bank statement, or the
       Charges and Cash Advances on the credit card statement, with the associated
       QuickBooks transactions.

> **Tip:**
> You can sort the columns in the *Reconcile* window by clicking the
> column heading. Sorting by amount may help you find
> transactions more easily.
>
> If you would like to change the columns displayed in the
> *Reconcile* window, click the *Columns to Display* button under the
> *Deposit and Other Credit* on the right side. This will allow you to
> select which columns you would like to see when you are
> reconciling.

12.   After you've marked all the cleared checks and deposits, look at the
       Difference field in the lower right corner as shown in Figure 10-3. It should
       be 0.00, indicating that your bank or credit card account is reconciled. If
       the *Difference* field is not zero, check for errors, as discussed in the next
       section.

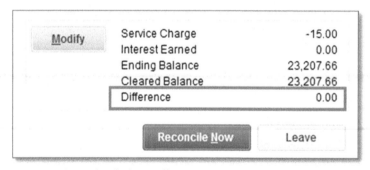

Figure 10-3 Reconcile, Checking Difference

> **Tip:**
> If you need to wait until another time to complete the
> reconciliation, you can click **Leave**. When you click **Leave**,
> QuickBooks will save your progress so you can complete the
> reconciliation later.

13.   If the *Difference* field is zero, you've successfully reconciled. Click **Reconcile Now**.

> **Note:**
> It is very important that you do not click **Reconcile Now** unless the *Difference* field is **0.00**. Doing so will cause discrepancies in your accounting records. Even a small discrepancy of $10 could be an error of $1,000 in deposits and an error of $990 in checks.

14.   The *Select Reconciliation Report* dialog box displays, as shown in Figure 10-4. The **Both** option is already selected, so click **Display** to view your reports on the screen.

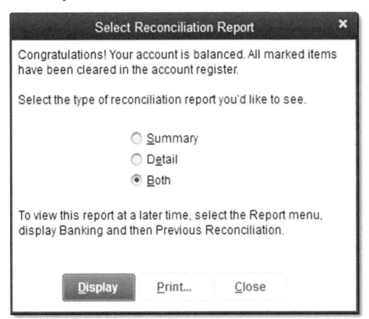

Figure 10-4 Select Reconciliation Report

15.   Click **OK** on the *Reconciliation Report* window

16.   QuickBooks creates both a *Reconciliation Summary* report and a *Reconciliation Detail* report. The length of the detail report will depend upon how many transactions you cleared on this reconciliation and how many uncleared transactions remain in the account.

17.   Print these reports for your records and close all open report windows.

Finding Common Bank Reconciliation Errors

If you have finished checking off all of the deposits and checks but the
Difference field at the bottom of the window does not equal zero, there is an
error (or discrepancy) that must be found and corrected. To find errors in
your bank reconciliation, try the following steps:

Step 1: Review the Beginning Balance Field

Verify that the amount in the *Beginning Balance* field matches the beginning
balance on your bank statement. If it does not, you are not ready to reconcile.
There are two possibilities for why the beginning balance will no longer
match the bank statement:

1. One or more reconciled transactions were voided, deleted, or changed since
    the last reconciliation; and/or,

2. The checkmark on one or more reconciled transactions in the account
    register was removed since the last reconciliation.

To correct the beginning balance discrepancy problem you have two options:

Option 1: Use the Reconciliation Discrepancy Report

From the *Begin Reconciliation* window, click on **Locate Discrepancies** as
shown in Figure 10-5. The *Previous Reconciliation Discrepancy Report* will
display on the screen.

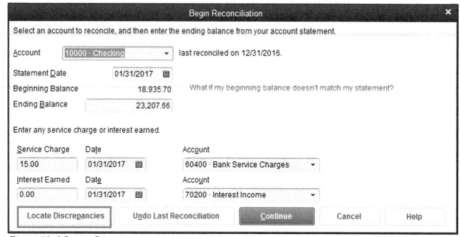

Figure 10-5 Locate Discrepancies

Review the report for any changes or deletions to cleared transactions. The *Type of Change* column shows the nature of the change to the transaction.

For each line of the report with "Deleted" in the *Type of Change* column, this indicates that a transaction that was previously marked cleared and reconciled was deleted. Re-enter the deleted transaction, then use the Bank Reconciliation window to re-reconcile the transaction that had been deleted.

For each line of the report with "Amount" in the *Type of Change* column, this indicates that a change was made in the amount of the transaction after it was marked cleared and reconciled. Double-click the transaction in the *Reconciliation Discrepancy* report to open it (i.e., QuickZoom). Change the amount back to the reconciled amount.

After returning all transactions to their original state (as they were at the time of the last reconciliation), you can then proceed to investigate whether the changes were necessary, and if so, enter adjustment transactions.

Option 2: Undo the Bank Reconciliation

The *Previous Reconciliation Discrepancy* report only shows changes to cleared transactions since your most recent bank reconciliation. If the beginning balance was incorrect when you performed previous bank reconciliations, the *Previous Reconciliation Discrepancy* report will not fully explain the problem.

If this is the case, the best way to find and correct the problem is to undo the previous reconciliation(s).

From the *Begin Reconciliation* window, click on **Undo Last Reconciliation** as shown in Figure 10-6.

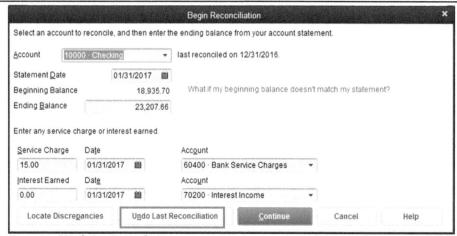

Figure 10-6 Undo Last Reconciliation

When you undo a reconciliation, QuickBooks resets your beginning balance to the previous period. However, the bank service charges and interest income that you entered in the prior reconciliation will remain in the check register and will not be deleted.

Therefore, do not enter bank service charges and interest income when repeating the bank reconciliation. Instead, clear those transactions along with the other checks and deposits when you re-reconcile the account.

Step 2: Locate and Edit Incorrectly Recorded Transactions

When you find a discrepancy between a transaction in QuickBooks and a transaction on the bank or credit card statement, you need to correct it. You will use different methods to correct the error, depending upon the date of the transaction.

Correcting or Voiding Transactions in the Current Accounting Period

If you find that you need to correct a transaction in QuickBooks and the transaction is dated in the current accounting period (i.e., a period for which financial statements and/or tax returns have not yet been issued), correct the error as described in the following paragraphs.

If You Made the Error

If you made an error in your records, you must make a correction in QuickBooks so that your records will agree with the bank. For example, if you wrote a check for $400.00, but you recorded it in QuickBooks as $40.00, you will need to change the check in QuickBooks. Double-click the transaction in the *Reconcile* window, or highlight the transaction and click **Go To.** Make the correction, and then click **Save & Close.** This will return you to the *Reconcile* window and you will see the updated amount.

If the Bank Made the Error

If the bank made an error, enter a transaction in the bank account register to adjust your balance for the error and continue reconciling the account. Then, contact the bank and ask them to post an adjustment to your account. When you receive the bank statement showing the correction, enter a subsequent entry in the bank account register to record the bank's adjustment. This register entry will show on your next bank reconciliation, and you can clear it like any other transaction.

Step 3: Determine if Error Is in Deposits or Checks

Determining if check or deposits are out of balance is a good way to start to understand where the bank reconciliation error may be. The bank statement provides totals for deposits and withdrawals as shown in Figure 10-7.

Summary of Your Business Checking Account	
Beginning Balance on 01/01/2017	$18,935.70
Total Deposits and other Credits	+ $45,415.89
Total Checks, Withdrawls, Transfers, and Account Fees	- $40,320.35
Ending Balance on 01/31/2017	$24,031.24

Figure 10-7 Bank Statement Summary

Use these totals from the bank to compare the totals on the lower left corner of the *Reconcile* window as shown in Figure 10-8.

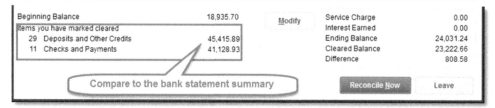

Figure 10-8 Reconciliation Totals

The cleared deposits in QuickBooks match the deposit summary from the bank. The checks are out of balance by $808.58, which happens to match the difference in the lower right of the *Reconcile* window.

Now that it has been determined that the difference is in the checks, sort by the amount column by clicking on the word *Amount* at the top of the column to see if that amount shows up.

As you can see in Figure 10-9, there is a check that was marked cleared for the amount of the reconciliation difference. After reviewing the bank statement and determining that this check is not shown on the bank statement, uncheck the check and the reconciliation will balance.

For period: 01/31/2017

Checks and Payments

✓	DATE	CHK #	PAYEE	AMOUNT ▲
	01/24/2017	5346	Sacramento C...	200.00
✓	01/05/2017	EFT	Merchant Servi...	450.18
✓	01/24/2017	5345	Chevron	465.71
✓	01/20/2017	EFT	Credit Union	497.55
	01/31/2017	5348	National Resta...	620.00
✓	01/17/2017	5340	Linen Supply C...	808.58
✓	01/17/2017	5342	Restaurant Su...	1,000.00
	01/24/2017	5344	Brand Manage...	1,000.00
✓	01/24/2017	5343	AT & T	1,158.16
✓	01/17/2017	5339	California Choi...	4,000.00
✓	01/24/2017	5347	State Board of ...	4,485.74
	01/31/2017	5349	Sysco	6,303.33

Figure 10-9 Checks Sorted by Amount

After unchecking the improperly cleared check, the difference in the lower right corner will be 0.00 and you can click **Reconcile Now** to complete the reconciliation and print reports.

Using Bank Feeds

The QuickBooks Bank Feeds feature allows you to download bank transactions into your QuickBooks file. Downloaded transactions save you time by decreasing manual entry and increasing accuracy. It is important to review each downloaded transaction to avoid bringing errors into your company file. Whether bank feeds are used or not, the reconciliation process needs to be completed each month, as described earlier in this chapter, to ensure that all transactions are accounted for.

QuickBooks uses a secure Internet connection and a high level of encryption when transferring information from your financial institution, but we do not provide any guarantees that information sent over the Internet is 100% safe from hackers. Use your discretion when deciding whether or not to use online banking. Bank fees may or may not apply. Check with your financial institution for their fee structure.

Bank Feed Setup

To begin to use Bank Feeds, you will need to set up the appropriate accounts to communicate with the bank. There are generally two ways to connect your bank and QuickBooks. "Direct Connect" allows for two-way communication with the bank so you can send and receive transactions. "Web Connect" allows you to download transactions only. Steps to set this up and fees vary by institution. To complete this process, refer to your financial institution's support department, the QuickBooks help files, or the videos in the *Learning Center Tutorials* located in the *Help* menu.

Downloaded Transactions

Once bank feeds are set up, you can download transactions from your financial institution by clicking the *Refresh* or *Download Transactions* button in the *Bank Feeds Center*, as shown Figure 10-10.

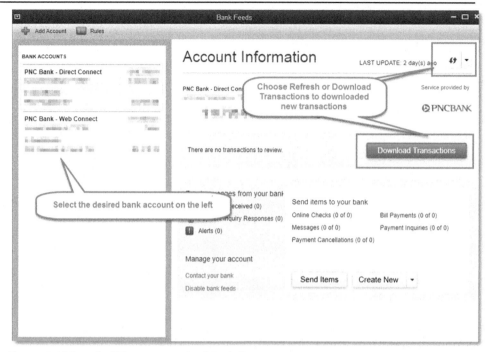

Figure 10-10 Download Transactions in Bank Feeds Center

All the new transactions from your financial institution will be listed in the *Bank Feeds Center* in the *Transaction List* as shown in Figure 10-11.

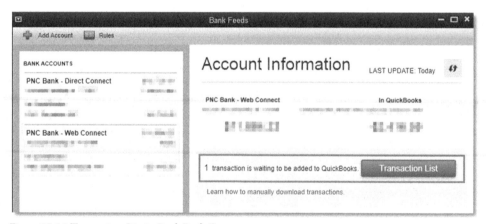

Figure 10-11 Transactions List in Bank Feeds Center

The transactions are now ready for review. Click on the *Transaction* List to display a list of downloaded transactions. As the transactions are downloaded, QuickBooks searches for similar transactions that have previously been entered. QuickBooks color codes the transactions based on whether it found a match, created a new transaction based on bank rules, or whether there is no match and no rule for the transaction as shown in Figure 10-12.

- Blue Transactions (Auto) indicate that an existing transaction is similar to the downloaded transaction, such as by having the same date and amount. You will want to review these to ensure that they are truly a match. If you have several transactions with similar dates and dollar amounts, they may not match perfectly. If a transaction is not a match, use *Action* on the right of the transaction and choose **Not a Match.**

- Orange Transactions (Changed) indicate that QuickBooks applied a *Rule.* Confirm that the rule was applied correctly and the correct *Payee* and *Account* are showing.

> **Note:**
> Rules are found by clicking the **Rules** button in the upper left corner of the *Transaction List* window. You can add or edit rules by opening the *Rules* and clicking **Manage Rules.** For more information on bank rules, press **F1** for help inside QuickBooks and search *Bank Rules.*

- Yellow transactions are bank transactions that are not found in QuickBooks and do not have any known rules to apply to them. You will need to review these transactions and enter the appropriate *Payee* and *Account.*

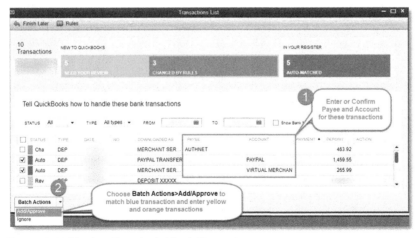

Figure 10-12 Matching Downloaded Bank Transactions

Processing Online Transactions

If you are able to establish two-way communication with your financial institution using Direct Connect, you will have the option to enter online transactions, such as online payments, bill payments, or transfers in QuickBooks and transmit instruction to the bank to carry out the payments. Contact your bank's online banking department for the specific transactions supported and fees that may apply.

Figure 10-13 displays an example of an online payment. You can create an online payment by opening the **Write Checks** window and checking **Pay Online**. Notice that there are some minor differences between a standard check form and an online payment form. For example, the check number field displays the word *SEND* until the transaction is sent to the bank, at which time the actual check number issued will be recorded.

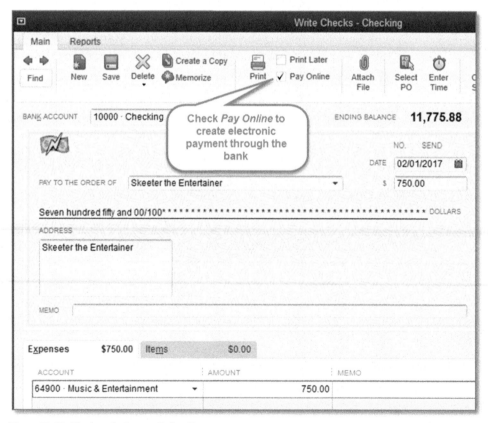

Figure 10-13 Checks to be Sent as Online Payment

If you are paying bills through the *Pay Bills* feature, you will select *Online Bank Pmt* as the payment method, instead of Check as shown in Figure 10-14.

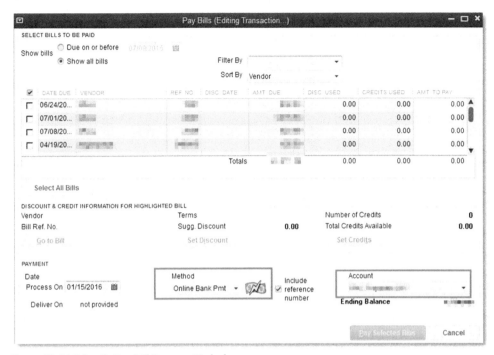

Figure 10-14 Select Online Bill Payment Method

After saving an online payment, the transaction is queued up in the *Bank Feed Center*. Figure 10-15 shows a recap of the items to be sent. By clicking the **Send Items** button in the *Bank Feed Center*, you can send the online payments and other online transactions, as well as download transactions from your financial institution.

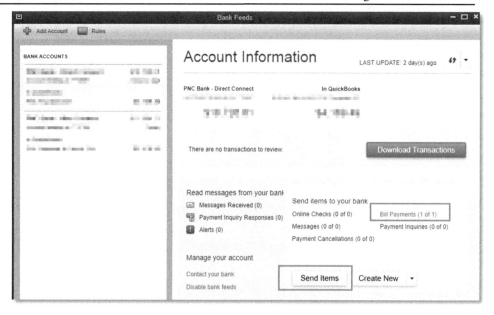

Figure 10-15 Sending Items in Bank Feeds Center

Your financial institution may require additional steps. Follow any guidelines given after clicking the **Send Items** button. For help with online banking connection issues, contact your financial institution.

Chapter 11
Reports for Restaurants

QuickBooks allows you to run standard reports or customize your own to get just the information you want to see, in the layout you prefer. Restaurant managers and owners will generally like to see their sales reports on a weekly basis, as opposed to a monthly basis, so they can compare sales across weeks. If the first of this month falls on a Friday and you run a report comparing this month to last month, this month may show much higher sales because there could be five Fridays included in this month's numbers. This chapter will show you how to customize some of the standard reports in QuickBooks to show results by week.

Memorized Reports – Overview

Customizing reports can take some finesse, but once you get a report just the way you want it, use the memorized reports feature to save your customizations so you don't have to reinvent the wheel each time you want to see the same report.

QuickBooks allows you to create report groups in the *Memorized Transactions List*. These groups can be for whatever you need them to be. You can create a group for *Weekly Reports, John's Reports, Restaurant Reports, Monday a.m. reports,* or whatever else you need a group for. Grouping makes it easy to run several reports at the same time.

In the restaurant sample file, we have grouped reports in the *Restaurant* group. This report group was created from the *Memorized Report List*.

To open the *Memorized Report List*, follow these steps:

1. Click on **Reports > Memorized Reports > Memorized Report List** as shown in Figure 11-1.

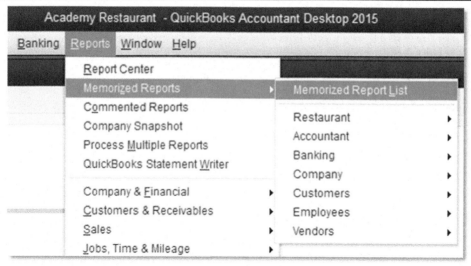

Figure 11-1 Memorized Report List

2. Click on **Memorized Report** in the lower left corner and select **New Group**.

3. Enter in the name of the group you would like to create.

4. Once the group is created, you will be able to add reports to it, which will be discussed later in this chapter.

In the restaurant sample file, there are several memorized reports that you can use to review and manage the business. These reports are accessible from the **Reports** menu, as shown in Figure 11-2. This chapter will go over some of the basic customizations that were used to create some of these reports. To see which customizations were applied to reports not covered in this chapter, open the restaurant sample file provided and follow these steps:

1. Open the report in question.

2. Click on **Customize Report**.

3. Click on the **Filters** tab. On the right hand side, the filters that were applied to that report will be displayed. We will discuss filters later in this chapter.

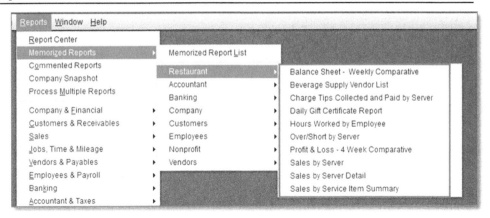

Figure 11-2 Memorized Reports Listing

Sales by Item Report

To view total sales for each item, create a *Sales by Item* summary by following these steps:

1. Click on **Reports** > **Sales** > **Sales by Item Summary**.

2. Change the dates to appropriate time frame by entering in the *From* and *To* dates or by clicking on the *Dates* drop-down on the left and choosing *Last Week*, *This Week*, *Last Month*, etc.

This report will show all of the items entered on the daily *Sales Receipt*, including *other charge, discounts, sales tax*, and *payment* items.

The report shown in Figure 11-3 is customized to include only *Service* items. By not including non-service items, the percent of sales is based solely on the food and bar sales, providing reports that are easier to measure across different time periods.

> **Did You Know?**
> All reports in QuickBooks have a *Customize Report* option which allows you to change which columns are shown (the *display* tab) as well as which information to include (the *filters* tab). The options change depending on the base report being customized.
>
> More information on building custom reports is included in our *QuickBooks Complete Textbook*, available at The Sleeter Group's online store.

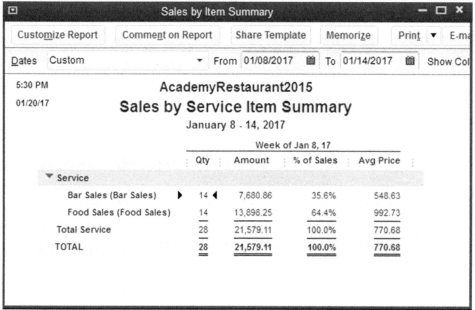

Figure 11-3 Sales by Service Item Summary

Figure 11-3 shows the total sales for the restaurant during the date range specified. The *Qty* column shows the quantity of daily *Sales Receipts* that were entered. The *Average Price* column is an average daily sales amount. It is calculated by dividing the total sales for that line item by the *Qty* column.

If a daily *Sales Receipt* entered for a server has zero for any of the line items for a particular day, this may cause calculation errors in your averages. Be sure to delete any lines that have zeroes, rather than leaving them on the form with a zero amount, to ensure the quantity is not skewed.

To compare totals of two time periods, change the dates to reflect the time period to be compared. In the *Show Columns* drop-down menu on the top of the report, select the time frame to display. Figure 11-4 shows a two-week period, totaled by week.

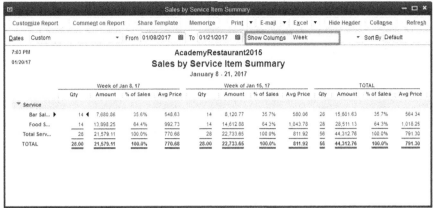

Figure 11-4 Sales by Service Item, 2 Week Comparison

Did You Know?

All QuickBooks reports can be exported to Microsoft Excel by clicking the **Excel** button on the top of the report and choosing *Create New Worksheet*. Once the report is in Excel, you can add and delete rows or columns, add formulas, and customize the report even further. For example, the report in Figure 11-4 could be changed to show the differences in the last set of columns, rather than the totals.

Sales by Server Report

To view total sales for each server during a data range, customize the standard QuickBooks report, *Sales by Rep Summary*.

To create the report shown in Figure 11-7, follow these steps:

1. Click on **Reports > Sales > Sales by Rep Summary**.

2. Change the dates to appropriate time frame.

3. Click on **Customize Report** on the upper left corner of the report as shown in Figure 11-5.

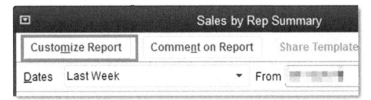

Figure 11-5 Customizing Reports

4.   By default, all items are included on this report, including gift certificates, tips, and other undesirable items. Click on the *Filters* tab and click the *Items* filter and select **All Services**.

5.   Click on the **Header/Footer** tab and change the report title to *Sales by Server* as shown in Figure 11-6 and click **OK**.

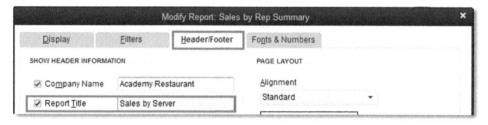

Figure 11-6 Customized Header for Sales by Server Report

This report shows total *Service* item sales for each server during the date range you specify and excludes gift certificates, tips, over/short, complimentary meals, and house charges.

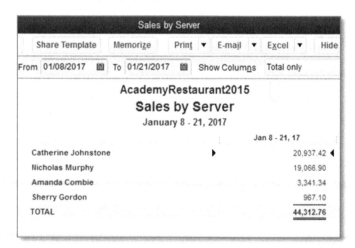

Figure 11-7 Sales by Server report

Did You Know?
Both standard reports and customized reports can be memorized in QuickBooks. Once you have customized a report, you can save the settings by clicking **Memorize** at the top of the report and saving it in the desired report group.

The *Sort By* column is to the right of *Show Columns.* By choosing **Total** instead of *Default*, the report will be sorted by the total sales column. By default the report sorts from lowest to highest total sales. Figure 11-8 shows the AZ button, which can be clicked to change the sort order.

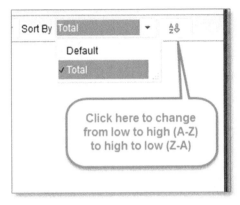

Figure 11-8 Sort By Drop-Down Menu Options

To take this report a step further, change the *Show Columns* drop-down menu selection from *Total Only* to *Week* to display columns of sales by server by week, as shown in Figure 11-9.

Sales by Server			
From 01/08/2017 🛗 To 01/21/2017 🛗 Show Columns Week			
AcademyRestaurant2015			
Sales by Server			
January 8 - 21, 2017			
	Week of Jan 8, 17	Week of Jan 15, 17	TOTAL
Catherine Johnst... ▶	9,811.91 ◀	11,125.51	20,937.42
Nicholas Murphy	7,458.76	11,608.14	19,066.90
Amanda Combie	3,341.34	0.00	3,341.34
Sherry Gordon	967.10	0.00	967.10
TOTAL	21,579.11	22,733.65	44,312.76

Figure 11-9 Sales by Server, by Week

Sales Detail by Server Report

To view a report of the sales details by server, including the day of the week, table count, and average sale, follow these steps:

1. Click **Reports > Sales > Sales by Rep Detail**.

2. Change the dates as desired.

3. Click **Customize Report** and choose the following columns on the *Display* tab: *Date, Num, Via, Count, Avg, Item*, and *Amount*.

4. Click the *Filters* tab and select *Item*. Change the selection to **All Services** to display the report shown in Figure 11-10.

5. Click the *Header/Footer* tab to change the *Report Title* to **Sales by Server Detail**.

6. Click **Memorize** at the top of the report to add this report to the desired report group.

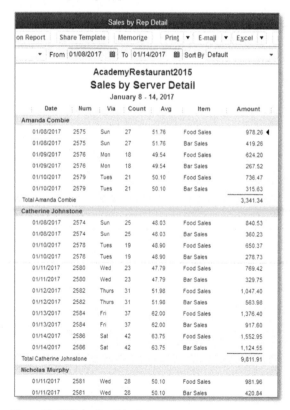

Figure 11-10 Sales Detail by Server report

The *Avg* column is the average of all sales for this server as entered on the daily *Sales Receipt*. To get the average Food Sales and Bar Sales, export the report to Excel and add a formula to calculate the average based on the *Count* column.

Over/Short by Server Report

In order to ensure that servers are not continually running over, or are short in their till, an *Over/Short by Server* report is included in the restaurant sample file. This report shows a day-by-day recap, by server, of the amount of the overages and shortages. Large amounts of shortages could indicate an employee is misappropriating funds by not turning in cash that she or he has collected. It could also be an indication that the server needs more training to ensure that they are making the correct change. We recommend reviewing this report regularly to spot any trends by server.

To run this report, start with the previously created report, *Sales by Server Detail*. If you have memorized this report and added it to the *Restaurant* group, it is simple to make a couple of changes and memorize the new report.

To create the *Over/Short by Server* report, follow these steps:

1. Click **Reports > Memorized Reports > Restaurant > Sales by Server Detail**.

2. Click **Customize Report** and remove these columns from the *Display* tab: *Count* and *Avg*.

3. Click the *Filters* tab and select *Item*. Change the selection to **Over/Short**.

4. Click the *Header/Footer* tab to change the *Report Title* to **Over/Short by Server**.

5.   Click **Memorize** at the top of the report. Since this report was previously memorized, a message is displayed asking if you want to replace or create a new report as shown in Figure 11-11

Figure 11-11 Memorized Report Exists, Replace or Add New

6.   Choose **New** and save the revised report in the *Restaurant* report group and click **OK**.

Tips Collected and Paid Report

The *Employee Tips Payable* clearing account should maintain a zero balance every day. In the event that this account does not zero out, the *Charge Tips Collected and Paid by Server* report will help you find the discrepancy. To view this report, run the memorized report included in the restaurant sample file called *Charge Tips Collected and Paid by Server* shown in Figure 11-12. Customize the date range as needed.

If each server's balance does not zero out every day, open the daily *Sales Receipt* entered on the day the imbalance was created and review the information posted to see if something was missed or entered incorrectly.

Sales by Rep Detail

Customize Report | Comment on Report | Share Template | Memorize | Print ▼ | E-mail ▼ | Excel ▼ | Hide Header

Dates Custom ▼ From 01/08/2017 To 01/14/2017 Sort By Default ▼

AcademyRestaurant2015

01/20/17

Charge Tips Collected and Paid by Server

January 8 - 14, 2017

	Date	Num	Via	Count	Avg	Item	Debit	Credit	Balance
Amanda Combie									
	01/08/2017	2575	Sun	27	51.76	Tips Collected - Credit Card		195.65	195.65
	01/08/2017	2575	Sun	27	51.76	Tips Out Liability	195.65		0.00
	01/09/2017	2576	Mon	18	49.54	Tips Collected - Credit Card		89.17	89.17
	01/09/2017	2576	Mon	18	49.54	Tips Out Liability	89.17		0.00
	01/10/2017	2579	Tues	21	50.10	Tips Collected - Credit Card		121.41	121.41
	01/10/2017	2579	Tues	21	50.10	Tips Out Liability	121.41		0.00
Total Amanda Combie							406.23	406.23	0.00
Catherine Johnstone									
	01/08/2017	2574	Sun	25	48.03	Tips Out Liability	144.09		-144.09
	01/08/2017	2574	Sun	25	48.03	Tips Collected - Credit Card		144.09	0.00
	01/10/2017	2578	Tues	19	48.90	Tips Collected - Credit Card		102.20	102.20
	01/10/2017	2578	Tues	19	48.90	Tips Out Liability	102.20		0.00
	01/11/2017	2580	Wed	23	47.79	Tips Collected - Credit Card		131.90	131.90
	01/11/2017	2580	Wed	23	47.79	Tips Out Liability	131.90		0.00
	01/12/2017	2582	Thurs	31	51.98	Tips Collected - Credit Card		193.37	193.37
	01/12/2017	2582	Thurs	31	51.98	Tips Out Liability	193.37		0.00
	01/13/2017	2584	Fri	37	62.00	Tips Collected - Credit Card		275.28	275.28
	01/13/2017	2584	Fri	37	62.00	Tips Out Liability	275.28		0.00
	01/14/2017	2586	Sat	42	63.75	Tips Collected - Credit Card		321.30	321.30
	01/14/2017	2586	Sat	42	63.75	Tips Out Liability	321.30		0.00
Total Catherine Johnstone							1,168.14	1,168.14	0.00

Figure 11-12 Charge Tips Collected by Server report

This report was created from the base report **Reports > Sales > Sales by Rep Detail**. The *Items* were filtered to only include *Tips Collected – Credit Card* and *Tips Out*. The *display* tab was modified to include only the columns you see in Figure 11-12. The *Via* column is the repurposed *Shipping Method* list used to capture the day of the week.

Gift Certificates Report

To view a report showing the sales and redemptions of gift certificates, run the **Daily Gift Certificate Report** in the restaurant sample file (Figure 11-13).

To run this report, start with the previously created report *Over/Short by Server* report and follow these steps to modify the report:

1. Click **Reports > Memorized Reports > Restaurant > Over/Short by Server**.

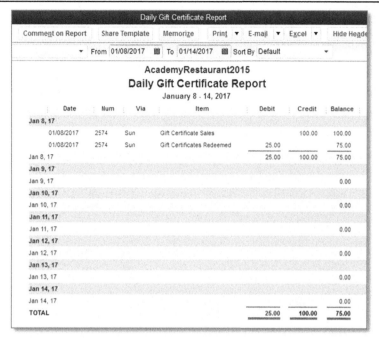

Figure 11-13 Daily Gift Certificate Report

2.   Click **Customize Report**

3.   On the *Display* tab, add the *Debit, Credit,* and *Balance* columns and remove
      the *Amount* column. This will make it easier to see the sales and
      redemptions in separate columns.

Did You Know?
You can search for column headers and filters by entering part of
the name in the *Search Columns* box or *Search Filters* box to
prevent the need to scroll up and down the list to find the
desired field.

---

4.   Change the *Total By* option on the *Display* tab to **Day**.

5.   Click the *Filters* tab and select *Item*. Change the selection to *Gift Certificate
      Sales and Gift Certificates Redeemed.*

6.   Click the *Header/Footer* tab to change the *Report Title* to **Daily Gift
      Certificate Report.**

7. Click **Memorize** at the top of the report. Since this report was previously memorized, click **New** to add this as a new entry on the *Memorized Reports List*.

Weekly Hours Worked Report

To view total hours worked by employee, by day, run the *Hours Worked by Employee* report included in the restaurant sample file.

To create this report, follow these steps:

1. Click **Reports > Jobs, Time & Mileage > Time by Name**.

2. Click **Customize Report**.

3. In the *Display* tab, modify the dates to the desired range, change the *Display columns by* option to **Day**, and change the *Display time grouped by* option to **Time by Name Only**, as shown in Figure 11-14.

> Note:
> The *Display Columns* option shown on the *Display* tab is the same setting as shown on the top of the report. It can be changed in either place.

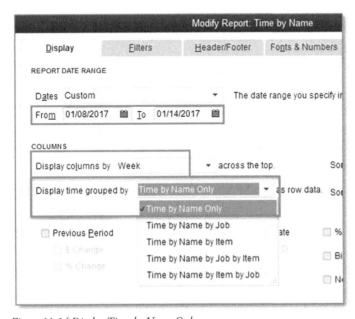

Figure 11-14 Display Time by Name Only

4. Click on the *Header/Footer* tab to change the *Report Title* to **Hours Worked by Employee**

5. Click **Memorize** at the top of the page to add this report to the desired report group.

Vendor Type List

If you added *Vendor Types* (as described on page 39) to the *Additional Info* tab of the vendor records, you can create a report to see all of the beverage supply vendors and their contact information.

The report in Figure 11-15 was created by customizing the *Vendor Contact List* report to include only the columns shown.

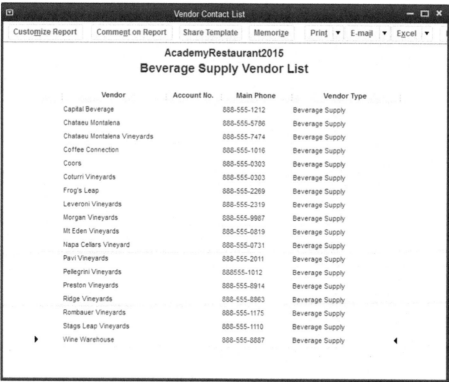

Figure 11-15 Vendor Type List

To change the vendor type, click on **Customize Report**, choose the *filters* tab, and select *Vendor Type* from the list of filters as shown in Figure 11-16.

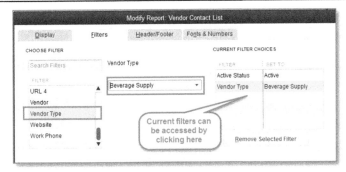

Figure 11-16 Vendor Type List, Change Filter

Displaying Multiple Memorized Reports

To create all or some of the memorized reports at once, follow these steps:

1. Open the *Memorized Reports List* by selecting the **Reports** menu and choosing **Process Multiple Reports** as shown in Figure 11-17.

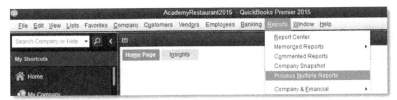

Figure 11-17 Process Multiple Reports menu item.

Select *Restaurant* from the list of memorized report groups as shown in

2. Figure 11-18.

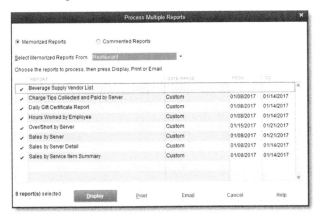

Figure 11-18 Restaurant Report Group, Memorized Reports

3. Select the reports to create on the left side with a check mark.

4. Review the from and to dates on the right side and make any necessary changes.

5. Click **Display** to display the selected reports on the screen. You can also choose *Print* or *Email* if desired.

6. To show the reports in the "cascade" layout, as shown in Figure 11-19, click on **Window > Cascade**.

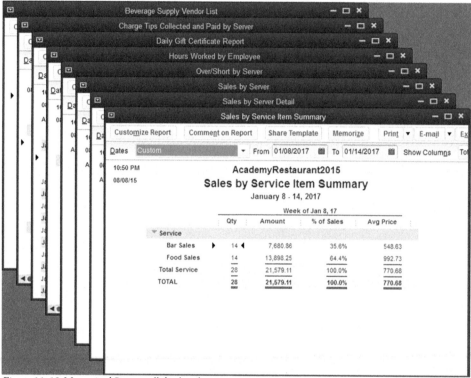

Figure 11-19 Memorized Reports all displayed on screen

> **Tip:**
> Be sure to close all these reports before exiting QuickBooks because leaving them all open will slow down QuickBooks' performance the next time you open the program.

Chapter 12
Understanding Financial Statement Reports

At the end of the week, month, quarter, or year, you can run the standard QuickBooks financial statement reports to see the overall financial condition of your restaurant. There are entire courses on understanding financial statements, but we want to give you a basic overview of what is included on the three main reports; Balance Sheet, Profit & Loss, and Statement of Cash Flows.

Balance Sheet

The Balance Sheet provides a snapshot of the restaurant at a particular point in time. It is a listing of all of the assets, liabilities and equity of the restaurant.

Assets are things of value that the business owns, like cash in the bank, accounts receivable (unpaid house accounts), inventory (unsold food), prepaid expenses (security or insurance deposits), fixed assets (equipment and leasehold improvements), goodwill, and other items of value such as the liquor license.

Liabilities are amounts owed to others, like accounts payable (unpaid bills), unpaid company credit card balances, gift certificates sold but not redeemed, sales tax due, unpaid payroll taxes, loans, and other debts of the restaurant.

Equity is the net worth of the business. Owner draws or distributions are reported here, as well as the current year profit (or loss) and accumulated profits (or losses) of the business since inception.

The report shown in Figure 12-1 is a weekly comparative Balance Sheet with a column for the change for the week.

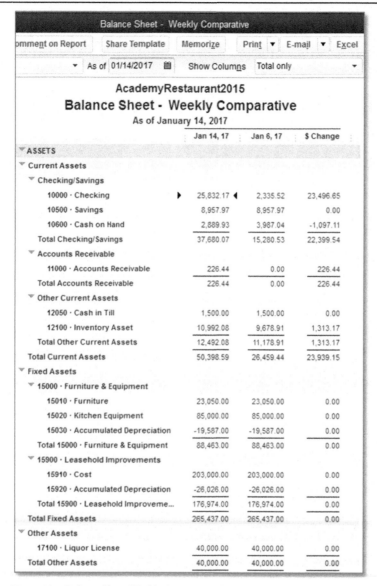

Figure 12-1 Balance Sheet, Weekly Comparative Report

To create this weekly comparative Balance Sheet, follow these steps:

1. Click on **Reports > Company & Financial > Balance Sheet Standard**.

2. Click on **Customize Report**.

3. Set the *Display* settings as shown in Figure 12-2. The dates are the week, month, quarter, or year to be analyzed.

4.   Check the boxes to add subcolumns for *Previous Period* and *$ Change*. QuickBooks will interpret the dates you entered in the date range and show the appropriate previous period on the report.

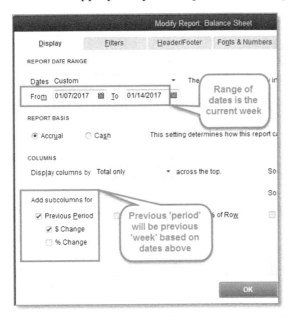

Figure 12-2 Display Settings for Weekly Comparative Balance Sheet

5.   Click on the *Header/Footer* to customize the *Report Title* to **Balance Sheet – Weekly Comparative**.

6.   Click **Memorize** to add this to the *Memorized Report List*.

The *$ Change* column shows the net change in the account for the time period. For example, Figure 12-1 shows the change in inventory that was calculated on page 125.

There are several financial ratios that can be used to analyze the financial health of a business using the information presented on the Balance Sheet. We will not go into them in detail, but you can research the Current Ratio, Quick Ratio, and Debt to Equity Ratio, to name a few. Regular monitoring of these ratios can help the restaurant see trends and the ratios can be compared to other restaurants using industry standards.

Profit & Loss Report

The Profit & Loss Report shows a snapshot of the restaurant for a *period* of time. It lists the sales, cost of sales, and expenses of the restaurant. The bottom line is called *Net Income* and is carried over to the *Net Income* line of the equity section of the Balance Sheet.

> **Note:**
> Net Income is needed in order to pay down loans or pay out owner draws. This is a distinction that many sole proprietors don't understand. They often think of the money they take as a "salary" (i.e., business expense), when it is actually a withdrawal of profits. Without profit, there can be no draws.

The income section shows all of the items the restaurant sells. Some prefer to have one line for *Food and Bar Sales* while others prefer to break them out. This is a restaurant-specific preference.

The cost of goods sold section shows all of the costs that go into the items sold. If you separate the income by food and bar sales, purchases and costs of goods for each category should be used so you can analyze food costs against food income, and bar costs against bar income.

The expense section shows all of the overhead-related costs of the business, like advertising, supplies, rent, repairs, and more.

To create a Profit & Loss report, follow these steps:

1. Click on **Reports** > **Company & Financial** > **Profit & Loss Standard**.

2. Set the date range on the report for the time period you want to analyze. Figure 12-3 shows calendar year 2016.

3. Click **Customize Report** and check the box for *% of Income* in the lower right corner of the *Modify Report* window. This displays the numbers as a percent of total income. This allows the restaurant owner to see trends in things like salaries or advertising as a percent of sales and compare them to industry averages. Be aware that cost of goods sold are not percentages of their corresponding income item, they are a percent of total income. To analyze food costs as a percent of food sales, a separate calculation is needed.

4. The 2016 report has been "collapsed," which is evidenced by the small arrows shown on *Insurance, Marketing Expenses, Payroll Expenses* and *Repairs and Maintenance*. To show the details of the subaccounts, click **Expand** in the upper right corner.

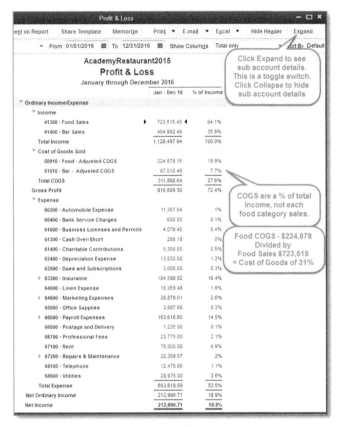

Figure 12-3 Academy Restaurant Profit & Loss for January 2016

5. After customizing the report, click **Memorize** to add the report to the *Memorized Reports List*.

QuickBooks reports are very customizable. To analyze the Profit & Loss report over several weeks, months, or quarters, set the date range for the start and end of the period and modify the *Show Columns* drop-down list to show by week, month, quarter, etc. This can be done on the standard or comparative reports.

If the restaurant uses a four-week reporting period, set the from and to dates to be the current reporting period, such as January 1-28, 2017, and in the

Display tab of the *Customize* window choose to show *Previous Period*, and QuickBooks will display the current four-week period and the previous four-week period of December 4-31, 2016. Figure 12-4 shows the display settings to create a four-week comparative Profit & Loss report. This report is included in the restaurant sample file as a memorized report.

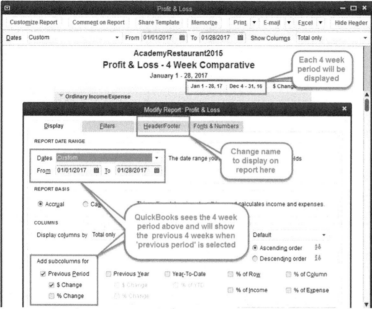

Figure 12-4 Week Comparative Profit & Loss Report

Statement of Cash Flows

The Statement of Cash Flows answers the question, "If we made that much money, where did it go?" Another way to think of it is as *Sources and Uses of Cash*. There are often items included in net income that don't translate to cash in the bank, such as a customer who charges a meal to a house account. The income is included on the Profit & Loss Report, but the money is not in the bank. The Statement of Cash Flows reconciles *Net Income* with cash at the end of the period. It also summarizes changes in the Balance Sheet accounts for the same period.

Net Income is the first line of the Statement of Cash Flows (Figure 12-5) and will be shown on the Profit & Loss Report for the same period. *Cash at end of period* is the last line and is shown on the Balance Sheet as *Total*

Checking/Savings. Everything on the Statement of Cash between net income and cash at the end of the period is either a "source of cash" (positive numbers) or a "use of cash" (negative numbers).

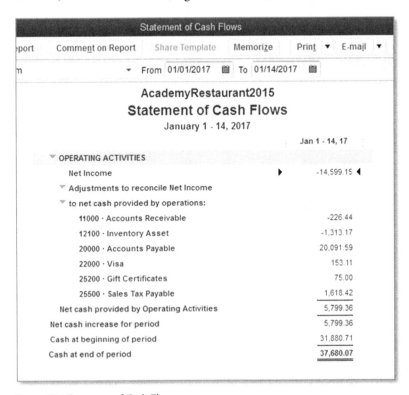

Figure 12-5 Statement of Cash Flows

Let's discuss the information shown in Figure 12-5 and the concept of sources and uses of cash in more detail.

- *Net Income* is a negative number, which indicates a loss. If nothing else happened, we would expect cash to decrease by the amount of the net loss. Conversely, if net income were positive, we would expect the bank account to increase by that amount. This never happens because there are always transactions that take place which need to be taken into account.

- *Inventory* increased for the period, which is a use of cash. This indicates that more items were purchased than were sold. The funds used to pay for the inventory came from money in the bank (or unpaid bills).

- *Accounts Receivable* shows a negative number. This happens when people eat at the restaurant, charge it to a house account, and don't pay the bill by the time this report is created. These invoices going unpaid are, in essence, a use of cash because we included this in our net income number, but we don't have the money yet. Conversely, if no house accounts were charged for the time period and customers paid off their balances instead, it would be a source of cash because money would be deposited in the bank that was not reflected on the Profit & Loss report.

- The increase in *Gift Certificates* is a source of cash because the money is in the bank account, but no income has been recorded. Income will be recorded when the customers redeem their gift certificates. If this number were negative (i.e., more gift certificates redeemed than gift certificates sold), it would be a use of cash because there would be income included on the Profit & Loss for which no money was received.

- The increase in *Accounts Payable* is source of cash. These are expenses recorded on the Profit and Loss report that have not been paid for yet. Conversely, if payables were paid down, this would show a negative number and it would be a use of cash because money would be coming out of the bank but not be reflected in the expenses.

- The increases in the *VISA* and *Sales Tax Payable* balances are sources of cash because these increases in liabilities were not paid for. This follows the same theory as the accounts payable example. If money was spent to pay down the credit card or pay down the sales tax balance, it would be a use of cash and shown as a negative number on the Statement of Cash Flows.

- Though not shown on this example, Owner Draws (which debit the Balance Sheet) are a use of cash. Money comes out of the bank that is not reflected on the Profit & Loss Report.

The underlying rule is that when a balance sheet account is debited (increase in assets or decrease in liabilities/owner's equity), it is a use of cash. When a balance sheet account is credited (increase in liability/owner's equity or decrease in assets), it is source of cash.

This can be a complex concept to understand, but once you understand the theory, it will help answer the question of where the profit went.

Chapter 13
Point of Sale Systems for Restaurants

Introduction

The previous chapters in this book have addressed the issues to consider related to accounting for your restaurant operation, and how to set up and record those transactions in QuickBooks. As discussed in Chapter 5, the Z-tape from the electronic cash register or the end-of-day report from a restaurant point of sale (POS) system reports the daily sales totals and payment receipts that will eventually be entered into QuickBooks. In addition to providing the operator with what was sold, when it was sold, by whom it was sold, and how it was paid for, a good POS system can help increase sales, optimize and streamline workflows, and improve guest service in your restaurant, which together will most likely produce an improved bottom line.

This chapter addresses how all of the above is achieved when a few pieces of hardware and software are set up and used properly. Whether you are a trusted advisor helping a client find a POS solution, or a restaurateur exploring the options, we hope to help you identify what features to consider and what questions to ask.

Hardware Considerations

Remote Printers

A remote printer is exactly what it sounds like it would be – a printer in a location that is different from the location of the terminal or workstation that sent the print job. Remote printers are typically used to inform line cooks and bartenders about orders they are responsible for preparing. Remote printers are strategically placed in the kitchen and bar where preparers can easily see the orders, and possibly near the expeditor who is responsible for coordinating delivery of prepared items to the table. What prints on the remote printer are the menu items ordered, with all of the preparation modifiers needed to prepare each item exactly as ordered, arranged in an order that makes sense to the preparer. The printout identifies which server placed the order, what table it is going to (including possibly the seat at the table), and the guest check number it is on, with the time the order was placed.

Imagine the additional attention a server can give to guests if that server rarely has to run to the kitchen and doesn't have to wait for drinks to be prepared at the bar. These types of solutions allow servers more time to inform guests about specials and house specialties, answer questions about menu items, suggest appetizers before dinner, recommend wine that compliments entrées ordered, sell desserts, and replenish beverages. Remote printers turn time running back and forth into time providing attentive service.

> Remote printers may be replaced or used in conjunction with display monitors. In some operations a display monitor may be more efficient than a printer. Display monitors are often used in fast food operations, in food prep areas, and for staging orders for drive-up windows.

Additional considerations and other benefits of utilizing remote printers are discussed in various other sections of this chapter.

Touchscreen Monitors

Servers are typically able to enter complicated orders more quickly with touchscreen monitors than with electronic cash register or computer keyboards. Less time operating the POS terminal creates more time to attend to other guest service needs.

Hand-held Devices

Hand-held devices used to facilitate order taking tableside can improve guest service. Orders entered tableside as the guest is ordering are more likely to be entered correctly and completely, especially if the server is prompted for choices included with the entrée when entering the order. Consider including hand-held order taking devices in your discussion with a potential POS vendor.

Customer Operated Kiosks

With kiosks, guests place their own orders which speeds up the order taking process. A kiosk may be an appropriate alternative in restaurants where the customer orders at a counter.

Software Considerations

The desired level of service and the menu items served in your restaurant operation will dictate some special needs your POS software must address.

Workstation and Remote Printer Configuration

The number of POS workstations and remote printers (if utilized), and the location of POS hardware, must be carefully considered to optimize and streamline workflows before choosing a POS system. There may be a need for more than one workstation at a high traffic location. A server standing in line to place an order at a workstation for any unreasonable length of time is wasting valuable service time. Restaurant POS software may operate a finite number of POS terminals and remote printers – there are often limits to the number of workstations and printers the software will accommodate. Make sure any system you consider can handle the hardware configuration you need today and anticipate in the future.

Menu Considerations

Touchscreen monitor and/or keyboard real estate is very valuable, as a carefully designed layout will facilitate finding menu items quickly, speeding up the order entering process. Monitor and/or keyboard layouts should be customizable to fit the menu served.

For restaurants that offer different menus at different times of the day, the ability to easily change the touchscreen or keyboard layout to reflect the menu that is served at that time of day is a desirable feature.

If your menu includes a build your own pizza with choices for crusts and toppings, and your system is driving remote printers, prompts for the choice of crust and toppings are necessary – and if choices are available by pizza quadrant, prompts for each quadrant are necessary. The same is true of any "build your own" menu item, such as a sandwich, omelet, or taco.

Software that will prompt for all options that accompany menu items is desirable for facilitating the order entering process. New menu items should not be allowed to be ordered until all required prompts for the previous menu item have been satisfied. An additional benefit of doing so is that servers become familiar with the restaurant menu more quickly because the software is constantly requiring the server to satisfy the prompts.

If your guests order menu items from a cashier, and then pick up the prepared items at a counter, your software needs to identify that order with the guest, either by adding their name to the order or with an order number.

Restaurants that include a mandatory service charge for larger tables need software to calculate and add that service charge to the guest check. Similarly, discounts, promos, loyalty programs, gift cards, etc. are other specialty needs to inform a prospective POS vendor about.

Multi revenue center operations that include a gift shop, snack bar, and/or rental shop need software that will handle the different transactions that take place in all of the revenue centers. Deposits for rentals might be a feature your POS system must address. Inventory management may not be necessary for the restaurant operation, but may be necessary for a gift shop.

Software Considerations with Remote Printers

Remote printers, as discussed above, may play a major role in improving service in a restaurant. A good POS system will include print options related to remote printers beyond what prints where. Software should not only allow options by menu item to print to a specific remote printer or more than one printer. Print options should include organizing the items printed in a user-defined order sequence, with the ability to collate like items. Print options should identify the server, table, and possibly the guest position at the table (to avoid food runners having to ask who ordered what when prepared food is delivered to the table).

When remote printers are used by cooks or bartenders to prepare items ordered, the preparer must be informed of all preparation details. Software that can prompt for those details when entering the order, using specific lists for prompts that must be satisfied and then allowing for optional modifiers to be added, will efficiently inform the preparer of everything needed to properly prepare the item. For example, suppose your menu has a cheeseburger on it, and included with the cheeseburger is a choice of French fries, sweet potato fries, or chips. Standard presentation includes lettuce, tomato, and raw onion. Ideally, when placing an order and selecting a cheeseburger, the server would first be prompted for temperature – a choice from a list of rare, medium-rare, medium, medium-well, and well done must be selected before continuing. Once a temperature is selected, a list of specific cheese choices the restaurant offers would appear. Once a cheese choice is selected, a list of sides, including French fries, sweet potato fries, and chips appears. Once the side is selected, optional modifiers such as no onion, no lettuce, no tomato, or add fried onions could be selected. New menu items ordered on the same guest check cannot be chosen until all required (mandatory) prompts for the cheeseburger have been satisfied. Again, the goal is to inform the preparer of everything the preparer needs to know to properly prepare the item, including the accompaniments included with that item, and to keep the server in the dining room and out of the kitchen.

Separate Checks

Regardless of how much guests thoroughly enjoy their dining experience as a result of the quality of the food, the excellent service, or the company and conversation, the entire experience can be ruined if paying the bill causes them to be late for their next event – or if separate checks are not an option. Ask your prospective POS vendor how easily one guest check can be split into several.

Reliability Considerations

As your restaurant POS system will most likely record the sale, manage service and workflows, produce the guest check, and perhaps process a payment by credit card, it must always be up and running. Once you depend upon your

POS system to do all of the above, imagine the chaos that will inevitably occur if it stops working for whatever reason. Both the hardware and the software must be reliable. Reliability may very well be the most important consideration for any POS system.

If you are looking at a Software-as-a-Service (SaaS) solution for your restaurant, a reliable Internet connection is critical. The Internet connection must have adequate bandwidth to allow the POS system to operate at maximum capacity without performance issues.

If your credit card processing system relies on the Internet to process payments, consider a backup manual process to accommodate taking payment from guests when credit card processing isn't possible.

All POS hardware should be plugged into power surge protectors that are plugged into dedicated power outlets. Verify that your restaurant is equipped with dedicated power outlets where POS hardware will be plugged in. If your restaurant is in an area prone to power outages, backup power generators might be considered.

Restaurant POS hardware is often operating in less than optimal conditions – for example in hot, greasy kitchens and by servers and bartenders with wet, sticky hands. In busy restaurants, hardware will take a beating. For that reason, all hardware must be commercial quality. Keyboards, if used, should be spill proof.

Hardware will occasionally break. Unfortunately, it tends to break at 7 p.m.on Friday night rather than 3 p.m. on Monday afternoon, and it doesn't warn you in advance. Local, reliable, and competent service should be available during the times you want it to be. A service contract for those times desired is recommended.

POS terminals and printers should be interchangeable. That is, if a terminal or printer stops working for whatever reason, it can be unplugged and quickly replaced by a spare, or by a terminal or printer that is moved from a less critical location. When hardware is moved, the software must be easily programmed to recognize the moved hardware in the new location, acting as if it were the original hardware it replaced. Remote printer destinations may need to be changed, and the software should easily facilitate doing so. For example, if remote printer #1 stops working and is replaced by remote printer #2, all items originally directed to remote printer #1 must now be re-directed to remote printer #2. Consider purchasing and storing a spare terminal, remote printer, and receipt printer, or developing a plan for operating when a piece of hardware decides to take the day off.

Reporting Needs

POS systems typically come with a variety of reports designed to provide management with the information it needs to make informed business decisions. While summary sales data will be entered daily into QuickBooks, management will rely upon the POS system to provide detail reports. Item sales reports, including best and worst selling items, and sales by the hour, are examples of reports typically desired by management. Determine what information is near and dear to your operation and ask a prospective POS vendor if their system will provide that information.

Labor reporting, including labor versus sales percentages by labor department, will require some sort of timekeeping mechanism within the POS software. At a minimum, employees might be required to clock in and select the task assigned to that employee for that time period, as restaurant employees often wear different hats on different days, or even on the same day. When clocking out, tipped employees might be prompted for the amount of tips earned during that shift, as there must be some mechanism for tipped employees to report tips earned, including shared tips. More information on tips can be found in the Tracking Tips chapter beginning on page 26, as well as the Customizing Payroll for Restaurants chapter beginning on page 51.

The ability to enter an employee schedule with start times and end times in the POS system, in order to report early and late clock ins and outs, is extremely valuable. A daily report showing missing clock ins and outs allows management to chase those missing punches before payroll processing day.

Assuming that the POS system will not integrate with QuickBooks, a report including sales, discounts, sales tax collected, tips, paid-outs, and settlements that can be used to record daily activity in QuickBooks is absolutely required. Ask a prospective POS vendor to show you an example of the report you will use to do so. Verify that the POS reporting system will provide the information needed to accurately record the daily sales activity, as described in Chapter 5.

If paid-outs happen regularly, there may be some value in recording them in the POS system, both to ensure that they aren't missed and to improve cashier accountability. When tips earned by servers are paid out on the day tips are earned, the ability to record those tips paid separately from other paid-outs helps to document exactly what was paid to the server, which is needed for processing payroll.

Server reports in the POS system can be very valuable to management. If the restaurant workflow includes server banking (guests pay the server rather than a cashier), a report showing cash to turn in is crucial. The same report might include sales information, including sales by menu item groups with quantities of menu items sold, identifying how successful the server is at selling appetizers, wine, beverages, and desserts. Excessive voids and refunds reported on the server report identify training issues on POS workstation operation.

A report showing open checks at any time of the day is critical for management and servers required to bank. Ideally, all guest checks will be settled before closing out the day.

We have identified methods for managing the sales tax reporting in QuickBooks beginning on page 115. However, if reports from the POS system are going to be relied upon to file the sales tax return, the POS system must report all the information necessary to do so. Servers will make mistakes ordering items and settling guest checks, including recording the proper amount of tip added to the guest check. Some reconciling must take place once the POS system has been Z'd out and the bookkeeper has reviewed the activity. The ability to correct a Z'd out sale is crucial to filing accurate sales tax and IRS Form 8027 information returns. If the restaurant is required to file an annual IRS Form 8027, ask a prospective POS vendor if their software will report charge sales and the charge tips added to guest checks settled by credit card or house charge. Also ask what other information relative to that form filing compliance is available.

> **Note:**
> IRS Form 8027 is *Employer's Annual Information Return of Tip Income and Allocated Tips*. It is required for businesses that normally employ more than 10 employees on a typical business day, when tipping is typical. Contact your tax advisor for more information on the filing requirements and whether or not this applies to your operation.

Gift Card and Loyalty Programs

Selling gift cards and encouraging guests to participate in a loyalty program present reporting challenges for POS systems. Ideally, gift cards can be created when sold and unredeemed gift card balances would be available to both the guest and management, perhaps even online. Similarly with loyalty programs, ideally an available reward earned would be automatically deducted from a guest check when it is finalized. Ask a prospective POS vendor if their system can handle your gift card and loyalty programs.

Security and Internal Controls

Safeguarding restaurant assets is a huge concern for any restaurant operator. Restaurant POS systems typically address security and accountability issues in some form or other, some better than others.

Inventory and cash are typically the two main asset safeguarding concerns, as there are great opportunities for both to disappear. While it is difficult for a POS system that does not manage inventory to protect inventory from mysteriously disappearing out the back door, it can help prevent it from disappearing out the front door. To ensure that no food is leaving the kitchen without being accounted for, all items served need to be on a guest check, whether paid for by a guest or not. The utilization of remote printers, together with a policy requiring menu items to be printed on a remote printer BEFORE preparation, ensures that the menu item is on a guest check somewhere. Comp items can be discounted, voided, or refunded to be removed from the guest check. A POS system that limits to management the ability to remove menu items outside of the current transaction only protects that menu item from being prepared and served without being paid for.

When remote printers are used, together with a policy that nothing is prepared until it prints on a remote printer, the ability for a server to serve something to a guest that isn't on a guest check is limited to the menu items the server prepares and serves without help (beverages, for example). If the quantity of beverages served (or anything that the server prepares and serves) is on a server report, the server report might identify the possibility of beverages that were served but not added to a guest check. At a minimum, the server report allows management to question low quantities of self-served items, which may help to keep a server honest.

Remote printers also ensure that proper prices are charged for menu items, including additional charges for substitute items and optional modifiers.

Server accountability concerns may be addressed by requiring servers to identify themselves when starting or recalling a guest check. That identity may be satisfied by entering a server number to start (a very low level of security) or by swiping a card with a magnetic strip that identifies the server or manager (a much higher level of security). Transferring guest checks from a bartender to a server or from server to server may best be limited to management.

Different permissions for servers, bartenders, managers, and timekeepers (typically kitchen help) may be desired. Programming roles may be limited to specific employees. Typically, programming is done in a different mode than normal guest check selling transactions, and requires permission to enter that mode. Programming mode should be limited to management.

Holding cashiers accountable for cash activity during their shift requires cashier reporting by the POS system. That can only happen if the cashier is identified prior to recording activity. Review sample cashier reports for any POS system you are considering.

Closing the day is typically done by a Z-out of the system. Security roles may limit this procedure to management. Typically, there is a number associated with each Z-out, sequentially advanced each time one is done. The bookkeeper might verify that today's Z-out number is only one greater than yesterday's, ensuring that multiple Z-outs aren't done during the day without reason. *Custom Fields* can also be added in QuickBooks, as described on page

36, and added to the daily *Sales Receipt* transaction, as described on page 64, to capture these sequential numbers.

Other Considerations

Integration

Although integrating a restaurant POS system with a general ledger package is not on our list of top considerations when choosing a POS system, integrating the POS system with other systems may be important. If your restaurant operation is located in a hotel, integrating with the hotel property management system may be important if hotel guests are allowed to charge restaurant purchases to their room.

Vendor Reputation

The reputation of a software vendor may be your first indication of how well a particular system will work for your operation. Ask the vendor to provide references of prior installations, then contact those references to verify how well the programming, training, and installation processes went for those installations. Find out how responsive the vendor is to service calls.

Training and Programming Issues

The amount of time it takes to learn how to use a POS system is critical if there is turnover in the staff that uses it. The more intuitive it is, the easier it is to learn. Well-designed keyboard layouts and/or touchscreen monitor layouts contribute to how intuitive it is to find menu items. Prompts for required modifiers contribute to the ease of training. Changing the description, price, and remote printer destination of a daily special, and changing menu item prices in general, shouldn't require a service call to the vendor or a two-year degree in computer programming.

Conclusions

When interviewing a potential POS vendor, start by showing the vendor your menus. Doing so will immediately provide the vendor with an understanding of your most basic needs. Indicate whether your operation includes table service or counter service or some combination of both. Decide if you want to utilize hand-held devices or kiosks for order taking, and remote printers for preparation. Address the number and location of workstations and remote printers. Address all reporting requirements and expectations you have in order to help manage the operation. Address all security concerns you have. Address the ease or difficulty of programming, including merely updating menu item prices. Address hardware and software reliability issues, and whether a service maintenance contract is available during the hours you would like it to be.

While price is always a consideration when choosing a POS system, don't be frustrated when a vendor cannot provide a price quote or perhaps even a ballpark price for his system quickly. There are far too many variables to accurately do so until the vendor is familiar with all your needs. The vendor may be able to provide a price range from prior installations – least expensive to most expensive – and what was included with those installations. This chapter has hopefully shown you how the right POS system for your operation may quickly pay for itself by tightening internal controls, optimizing and streamlining workflows, improving customer service, and increasing sales.

We hope you now have confidence in your ability to talk intelligently with, and to question, a potential POS vendor about their system in order to determine if it is the right system for your operation.

Appendix A
Create New Company File from Sample File

You can use the information contained in this book to set up your company file completely from scratch, or you can use the restaurant sample file to export certain lists and templates to make the setup go a little quicker.

To use the restaurant sample file to export lists and templates, start with a fresh restore of the restaurant sample file as discussed on page x. After you have the restaurant sample file restored, the new company can be created.

To create a new company file, open QuickBooks and follow these steps:

1. Select **File > New Company**.

2. Choose **Express Start** as shown in Figure 13-1.

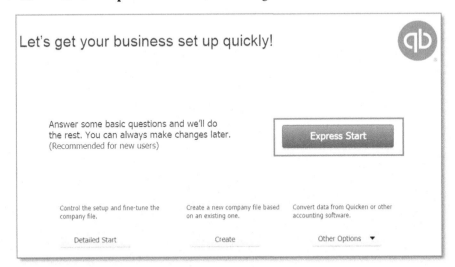

Figure 13-1 Express Start

3. QuickBooks will ask you for basic company information as shown in Figure 13-2.

4.   Enter in the *Business Name*.

5.   In the *Industry* field, click **Help me choose**. Scroll down to the bottom of
      the list of industries and choose **Other/None**. Resist the temptation to
      choose Restaurant/Caterer because choosing anything other than
      Other/None will create an undesirable *Chart of Accounts* list. Since you are
      importing the *Chart of Accounts* from the restaurant sample file, you need to
      start with a bare bones, basic *Chart of Accounts* provided with the
      Other/None industry.

6.   In the *Business Type* filed, select the appropriate business type for this
      restaurant (sole proprietor, corporation, etc.).

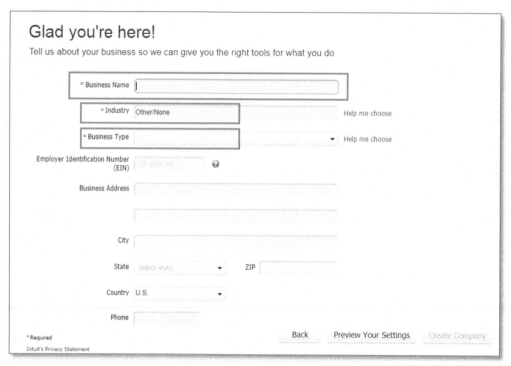

Figure 13-2 New Company Information for Express Start

7.   Fill in the additional information and click **Create Company**.

8.   Select **Start Working** to open the newly created QuickBooks file. The rest
      of the details will be added later.

The next steps will be to export the lists and templates from the restaurant
sample file and import them in to the newly created company file.

Export Lists from Sample File

To export a list follow these steps:

1.   Open the restaurant sample file that you previously restored by clicking **File > Open Previous Company** and selecting **AcademyRestaurant2015**.

2.   Select **File > Utilities > Export > Lists to IIF Files** as shown in Figure 13-3.

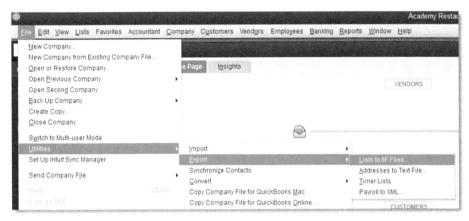

Figure 13-3 Export Lists to IIF Files

3.   Choose the list you would like to export and save it in a location you will be able to find easily. We recommend selecting one list at a time and saving each as a separate file.

> **Note:**
> The Chart of Accounts, Sales Tax Code List and Items List are the most important lists you will need to export. You will want to create your own Vendor List, Customer List, and Employee List. Other lists, like the Payment Terms List, are easily created using the methods described in this book. Payroll Items cannot be exported and must be created from scratch.

4.   Export each of the lists you will need (Chart of Accounts, Sales Tax Code List, and Items List) from the restaurant sample file so you won't have to go back and forth after importing each list.

5.   Close the restaurant sample file.

Import Lists to New Company File

There is a specific order that needs to be followed when importing lists because some lists rely on information contained in another list. The *Items List* must be imported after the *Chart of Accounts* and *Sales Tax Code List* because the *Items List* relies on information contained in both of these lists.

We recommend you import your lists in this order:

- Chart of Accounts

- Sales Tax Code List

- Items List

If you are importing any additional lists, be sure to import them in the correct order to ensure that any information needed for the particular list is already in your new company file.

To import an IIF files into your new QuickBooks file, follow these steps:

1. Open the new company file by clicking on **File > Open Previous Company** and selecting the company file you created on page 181.

> **Tip:**
> Create a backup of your company file in case there is a problem with the import, you can restore to the version that existed before you started the import. For more information on making a backup, press **F1** inside QuickBooks and search for **back up company files.**

2. Select **File > Utilities > Import > IIF Files**.

3. Locate the exported file on your local hard drive and choose **Open**.

4. After importing the lists, QuickBooks displays a message that your data has been imported, as shown in Figure 13-4.

Figure 13-4 Data Imported Successfully

Repeat the steps above for each list that needs to be imported.

> **Note:**
> After importing the *Items List* you will need to delete or edit the *CA Sales Tax* item to reflect your particular needs, including the name of the item, tax rate, and tax agency to which you pay the sales tax, as discussed on page 34.

Additional Setup and Modification

Setup Preferences

In order to activate certain features in QuickBooks, set up the *Preferences* as discussed on page 5 in the Setting up QuickBooks for Restaurants chapter.

Modify Chart of Accounts

The imported *Chart of Accounts* may require modification. Feel free to add, edit, or delete accounts to ensure that the list is complete for your particular needs. Refer to page 14 for more information.

Review the Items List

Click on **Lists > Items List** and review the list to ensure that it contains all of the items you will need for your restaurant. Add any additional *Service, Other Charge, Discount, Payment*, or *Sales Tax* items, and edit/delete items that don't make sense for you. Refer to page 21 for more information.

Custom Fields

The templates in the restaurant sample file include the use of *Custom Fields*. Before importing templates, ensure that all of your custom fields have been set up as described on Page 36.

Additional Setup

Set up *Sales Reps* as described on page 35.

Continue with the rest of the setup as described in this book.

Exporting Templates

As in the case of lists, templates are exported and imported individually. To export templates from the sample data file, follow these steps:

1. Open the restaurant sample file as described on page 183.

2. Open the *Templates* list by click on **Lists > Templates**.

3. Click on the **Restaurant Daily Sales** template.

4. From the lower right corner of the *Templates* window, choose **Templates** and click **Export**, as shown in Figure 13-5.

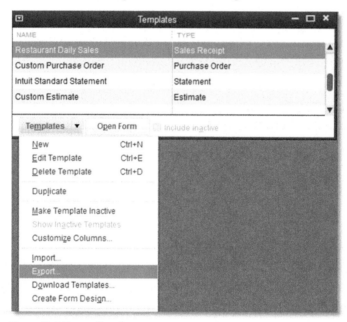

Figure 13-5 Export Template

5. QuickBooks exports the file with the same name and a **.DES** extension.

6. Save the file in a location that you can locate easily and choose **Save**.

Now that the file has been exported, it is ready for import into the new company file.

Importing Templates

We can't stress enough how important it is to ensure that any custom fields used on the templates are set up in the new file prior to importing.

To import a template, follow these steps:

1. Open the restaurant sample file as described on page 183.

2. Open the templates list by clicking on **Lists > Templates**.

3. In the lower left corner, click on **Templates >Import.**

4. Find the template you would like to import on your local hard drive and click **Open**.

5. QuickBooks will open the selected template and automatically take you to the *Basic Customization* window.

6. From the *Basic Customization* window, click **OK** to save the template.

You are now ready to use the methods describe in this book.

About the Authors

Doug Sleeter

Doug Sleeter (@dougsleeter) is a passionate leader of innovation and change in the small business accounting technology world. As a CPA firm veteran and former Apple Computer Evangelist, he has melded his two great passions (accounting and technology) to guide developers in the innovation of new products and to educate and lead accounting professionals who serve small businesses.

Doug has been named one of the "Top 25 Thought Leaders" by *CPA Practice Advisor* for several years, as well as one of *Accounting Today's* "Top 100 Most Influential People in Accounting" from 2008 through 2015. He was recently awarded the Small Business Influencer Champion award. Doug is the founder of the Sleeter Group, author of numerous books, and writes regular columns for the *Sleeter Report* and *CPA Practice Advisor*. Doug and his family live in Pleasanton, California.

Stacey L. Byrne, CPA

Stacey Byrne (@SLByrneCPA) is a practicing CPA with 25 years' experience consulting with a variety of small to medium-sized businesses including restaurants, construction companies, law firms, and not-for-profit organizations. She has worked as a staff accountant at the Iacopi, Lenz & Co. CPA firm, and is the former director of finance for a

management company where she oversaw accounting and payroll for multiple facilities, including a sports/entertainment arena, theatre, ice rink, and ballpark. Stacey is a former adjunct professor of QuickBooks at San Joaquin Delta College in Stockton, California.

Stacey holds several Intuit certifications in QuickBooks (Advanced Desktop, Advanced Online, and Enterprise). She is a certified Sleeter Group QuickBooks consultant and a certified Xero Partner.

Stacey holds a B.S.B.A. degree in Accounting from California State University, Stanislaus, and is currently in pursuit of her M.S. Ed. degree in Online Teaching and Learning at California State University, East Bay. She is also a member of several professional organizations, including the California CPA Society, Sleeter Group Consultants Network, and the Woodard Network.

When she is not writing, working with clients, or studying, you will likely find Stacey at a San Francisco Giants game or enjoying family time with her two sons.

Other Resources

References

For further study and reference about the topics in this book, consult the following resources:

1. The Sleeter Report online blog
   www.sleeter.com/blog

2. Find a Sleeter Group Certified QuickBooks Consultant
   www.sleeter.com/user/consultant/search

3. *QuickBooks Consultant's Reference Guide* by Doug Sleeter

4. *QuickBooks Complete Textbook* by Doug Sleeter

5. *Grow Your Accounting Practice Using Bill.com* by Judie McCarthy

6. apps.intuit.com for third party programs that integrate with QuickBooks

7. IRS Publication 3144 about Tips and Tip Reporting

8. IRS Form 4070 Employee's Report of Tips to Employer

9. IRS Tax Topic 761 Tips - Withholding and Reporting

10. IRS Form 8846 Credit for Employer Social Security and Medicare Taxes Paid on Certain Employee Tips

11. IRS Form 1099-MISC instructions for rules on reporting certain payments made in the course of business

12. IRS Form W-9 Request for Taxpayer Identification Number and Certification

13. For rules for reporting tips to remain in compliance we recommend this article by Bonnie Lee, EA
    smallbusiness.foxbusiness.com/finance-accounting/2012/08/16/how-business-owners-can-write-off-employee-tips-and-meals

14. Bonnie Lee, a Small Business Tax expert, columnist for *Entrepreneur Magazine*, and the Author of *Taxpertise, The Complete Book of Dirty Little Secrets*, available at www.taxpertise.com.

Index

CPSIA information can be obtained
at www.ICGtesting.com
Printed in the USA
LVOW06s1825280817
546690LV00032B/555/P